Praise for *The Broke Diaries* by Angela Nissel

"The best book I'   Chris Rock

"Charming and sharp, Nissel's diary will be relished by anyone who's ever been a student and remembers those ramen
noodles."   —*Publishers Weekly*

"Being tapped out sucks, but the deft way Nissel transforms
the ordeals of poverty into funny, reassuring anecdotes
makes it an almost enviable condition."   —*Mademoiselle*

"Nissel's sassy, snappy voice . . . easily carries the full lightness
of this unpretentious book."
                        —*The Village Voice Literary Supplement*

"What makes Nissel's book shine is her unsentimental prose
and wicked sense of humor."   —*USA Today*

"*The Broke Diaries* is, as Nissel so aptly puts it, the Encyclopedia
Broke-itannica."   —Raleigh-Durham *Independent Weekly*

"[Nissel's] searing laugh-out-loud commentary makes this a
must have—if you're broke yourself, get it from the library."
                                    —Honeymag.com

"Angela Nissel offers her heartbreaking, humorous and dead-
pan look at her life as a college student in the refreshingly
candid *The Broke Diaries*."   —*Essence*

"As funny as *The Broke Diaries* is, as quick-witted and self-reliant as the heroine emerges, the book can also be read . . . as an indictment of a system in which it's too easy for a working-class student to slip through the cracks."

—*The Philadelphia Inquirer*

"Nissel's personal voice . . . shines through each entry [with] her cynical, edgy, yet lighthearted tone." —*Hip Hop Congress*

"[*The Broke Diaries*] had me cracking up laughing out loud to the point where my kitten jump[ed] in the middle of the book just to see what's so darn funny." —*Sister 2 Sister*

"Nissel writes with absurd wit and candor." —*Insite* (Atlanta)

"Full of clever dialogue and witty entries . . . [*The Broke Diaries*] will have you laughing out loud." —*Black Issues Book Review*

"Nissel's perspective is . . . refreshing." —BlackPlanet.com

"Angela has a really off-the-wall sense of humor, and what makes it even funnier is it's true."

—Aaron McGruder, *The Boondocks*

MIXED

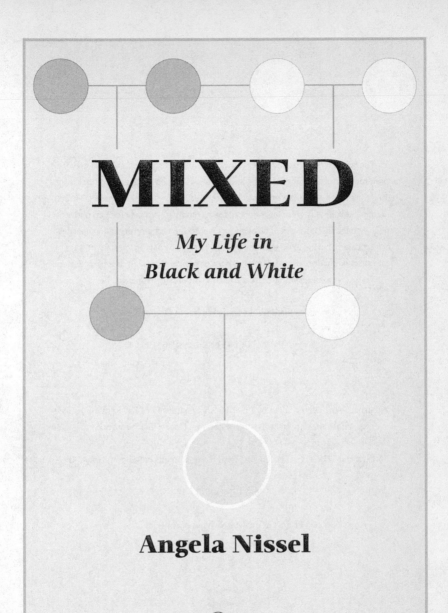

MIXED

My Life in
Black and White

Angela Nissel

Villard ⓥ New York

The characters in this book are real, but it bears mentioning that I have used pseudonyms for a number of them, and in a few cases I have gone a step further by altering their descriptions (for example: in the book I imply that my husband is attractive, when in truth, he is frighteningly ugly and when company visits I hide him under the bed). Though this is a work of nonfiction, I have taken certain storytelling liberties, particularly having to do with the timing of events. Where the narrative strays from strict nonfiction, my intention has been to remain faithful to the characters and to the essential drift of events as they really happened.

A Villard Books Trade Paperback Original

Published in the United States by Villard Books, an imprint of The Random House Publishing Group, a division of Random House, Inc., New York.

VILLARD and "V" CIRCLED Design are registered trademarks of Random House, Inc.

ISBN 0-345-48114-3

Printed in the United States of America

www.villard.com

2 4 6 8 9 7 5 3 1

Book design by Mercedes Everett

For Reuben

Contents

MIXED

White Thug, Black Panther

"Mom, how did you and Dad meet?" I asked my mother over the phone. It was close to her bedtime. I was praying she was drowsy so I could catch her off guard.

"Reverend Rob says hi," my mother replied, in a tone that meant *my man is sitting next to me, so I'm not going to talk about your father.*

It always happens. I bring up my father, and suddenly my mother's favorite Lifetime movie is on or her fiancé is there and she just has to catch me up on how his mortuary classes are coming along.

"Guess what he told me? The more fat you have, the more slowly you decompose," she continued.

It's not that I don't love hearing about Reverend Rob's adventures in the death-care industry, and I'm certainly glad my mother has found love after thirty years of being single. She and Reverend Rob make an adorable couple. He's five foot four; my mother is five foot zero. I'm taller than both of them, and looking down at the sight of them in tiny love is so cute, sometimes I have to restrain myself from patting them on their heads. It's like you could just stick them on top of their own wedding cake and serve it.

I know my mother doesn't enjoy talking about my father, especially in front of her fiancé. It took months before she even felt comfortable telling him that her ex-husband was a white man.

"I'm a little worried what he's going to think," she said to me, about a week before she confessed her vanilla sin. Reverend Rob wasn't shocked; he just laughed and pointed to a picture of my mother, my brother, and me. "Come on, now," he said. "Unless you adopted your kids, that's pretty obvious."

My husband and I are the same race (African American and everything else except Asian), the same religion, and lived less than two miles from each other, yet it took us one-year subscriptions to Match.com and six months of e-mails and chatting before we met. If it took all that for us to find each other, how in the world did my mother, a Black Panther from West Philly, meet and marry a white guy from a small town in upstate Pennsylvania? I don't even think my father had black people in his hometown; I remember being six years old and taking long rides to visit his relatives.

"Where are the sidewalks?" I asked my mother from the backseat of our Ford Granada.

"I don't know," she said. "They seem to just disappear once you get out of the city, don't they?"

"Where are the black people?" I asked, later on in the trip. She gave me the same answer she had for the sidewalks.

I gave up on probing into my mother and father's dating life that evening and called a few weeks later. After listening to details of Reverend Rob's latest mortuary lesson (bargain coffins may not be such a bargain), I tried a slight variation on my original question about my mother and father's romance.

"Mom, what did you think of Dad when you first met him?"

"I thought he was black," she replied.

Oh. My. God. Who approved my mother's Black Panther application? If she couldn't tell the difference between a black man and a white man, how effective could she have been at fighting *the*

Man? How could she ever think my green-eyed, freckle-faced, sandy-haired father was black? He's so pale that my mother's post-divorce code name for him was Master Alabaster, as in "Girl, I have to go to court again. Master Alabaster hasn't paid child support for six months, but I saw him driving a brand-new car."

There was silence on my mother's end of the line. I started laughing so hard I coughed and had to throw down the phone for a moment to compose myself.

"You okay? Get some water! Get some water!" my mother, always the nurse, yelled through the receiver.

"How could you think he was black?" I choked out between laughs.

"What do you mean, How could I think he was black? He lived on *my* block!" my mother said, and started laughing herself. "There were no white people except his mother for miles around! He had a black stepdad, and all his friends were black. I just thought he was mixed and came out really light." Her voice lowered. "I was naïve, I guess. I was naïve about a lot of things.

"To be sure about his race, I asked him about it on our first date. He had taken me to an oldies night, and we were dancing. In the middle of one of our dance moves, I just came out and asked him, 'Are you white?' He said, 'Yep.' He told me he was born in an all-white town in Pennsylvania and moved to West Philly when his mother got remarried to a black man.

"I thought, Oh, Lord, what have I gotten myself into? We kept on dating, though. People looked at us like we were crazy. I had a very big Afro and a very white man on my arm.

"You have to understand, I worked for the Black Panthers in their free clinic as a nurse *and* I worked for the Medical Committee for Human Rights. I probably have an FBI file; I was *deep* into Power to the People. Some folks didn't understand how I could be with your dad. People had a misconception that Black Panthers hated all white people. They didn't understand that I could fall in love with a white man and still work for social justice.

"The people who were the most vocal about us dating were the black men. Black men would shout right at me, 'You trying to look black with your big Afro, but you're not black!' "

My mother stopped talking. Maybe she was thinking of the guys who judged her for being with a white guy; perhaps she was figuring out that their disapproving reactions were why it took her so long to tell Reverend Rob that her ex-husband is white. Or maybe she was wondering why she didn't run off and be with a black man when she had the chance. Once, when my mother found out my father was cheating on her, I heard her on the phone crying to her best friend, "I knew I should have married that African prince in college! He was good to me, and he was rich! He took me to Macy's and told me to pick out anything I wanted!"

Later that day, I informed her that if she had married the prince, she wouldn't have been blessed with me (conceited at eight years old!). My mother's face dropped with the realization that I had overheard her conversation. She put her hands on my shoulders and said she wouldn't give me up for anything in the world, not even to be an African princess with a high-limit Macy's account.

Faced by my mother's silence, I had to think of a question that would lead her to tell a story. My mother will spill her guts about anything as long as she gets to tell a long, animated story while doing it. She sometimes preaches the children's sermon at her church, and all week leading up to Sunday, she practices her storytelling choreography in front of a mirror. Her arms flail at her sides as she pretends she's outrunning and ducking imaginary sins. She sometimes recites her own poems to the children, the subject matter of which is often black pride. I remember a pastor coming up to her after a particularly Afrocentric sermon. "*You* used to be married to a white man?" he asked. "I just don't believe it."

"Mom, what did Dad do when black guys would step to you about being with him?"

My mother laughed again. I heard her rise from her sofa to start the story. "Your father was crazy. He'd be all up in their faces, trying to fight them. More than one date ended with me saying, 'Jack, please. Let's just go.'

"Of course, no one could believe I actually married the white man, but the biggest shocker was when I had you. I was head nurse at the city hospital back then, so I knew nurses all over town. I knew some in Pennsylvania Hospital, where you were born. Some of the nurses there hadn't seen me in years and only knew me as this militant Black Panther.

"When I was in the hospital recuperating from having you, this nurse who knew me from college saw how white you were and checked the wristband three times before she gave you to me. I had to say 'Yes, this is my baby' many times during the days after you were born."

My mother started laughing again, then yawned. I told her to go to sleep, but she ignored me. No story goes unfinished with her, especially if she's not paying the long distance charges.

"I had to share a room with a white lady, and she was not too happy about my chocolate butt being in the room with her. She wouldn't even speak to me. Soon after they brought her in, her electric hospital bed started folding up, with her and her baby in it. She had just had a C-section and couldn't move too well, so I grabbed her baby and snatched the plug out of the wall to make the bed stop folding up on her. Then she had the nerve to start screaming like I was trying to steal her baby and didn't even thank me for getting her baby out of the bed.

"As if on cue, your dad walks in to see how I'm doing. The white lady still hadn't recovered from the shock of being eaten by her own hospital bed, and then in comes a white man to kiss me on the lips! That lady looked like she wished the bed would eat her back up again.

"When your dad left, she was steaming. Then one of the big doctors at the hospital comes in to see me. We had both volunteered at the Human Rights Committee together. He nods to her, and goes by her bed, walks right up to me, and says, 'Hey, Gwen, you still head nurse at City?' Her eyes got so big. Her whole world changed that day.

"The next day, I said good morning to the woman and she wouldn't say anything back. So later, a nurse came in while I was holding you and asked your name. I said, 'Angela'; then, loudly, I added, 'After Angela Davis!' just to make her think she was sharing the room with a radical.

"But that wasn't right. I didn't name you after Angela Davis. I named you after I saw your face. You looked just like an angel, and I knew there was no other name I could give you."

Damn, I kinda wanted to be named after Angela Davis. Oh, well.

I heard my mother's microwave go off. The beep seemed to jolt her out of reminiscing. Her voice lowered. "I have to go," she said.

"Okay," I said, a little saddened at the abrupt ending. Hearing the disappointment in my voice, she perked up.

"Did I tell you I'm on Weight Watchers again? I get weighed in tomorrow. I'll call and let you know how much I've lost! If I could get back down to the size I was when I had you, I'd be a foxy mama!"

"Okay, good night, foxy mama," I replied, hanging up the phone and reminding myself to update my mother's slang on my next visit home.

After I hung up, I wondered if there was a Black Panther alumni newsletter and if my mother had recently sent in an update.

Gwen Nissel '74 writes to say that she regularly chats about Weight Watchers points with her half-white daughter. Though she no longer actively participates in the revolution, she is happy to announce that the divorce from the white man finally went through and she is now engaged to a black Baptist preacher.

Primary Colors

1992: The Crayola Company introduces sixteen-count Multicultural Crayons. These crayons "give a child a realistic palette to color the people of the world." 　　　　　　　　 *—Crayola.com*

In the late seventies, before I started grade school and my parents were still semihappily married, life as a mixed kid seemed pretty simple. Until the outside world started pointing it out to me, I didn't even know that having parents of different races was unusual. Once I started school, my mother took on the task of helping me prepare for possible outside racist forces. She phrased her lessons like she worked for the Biracial Marketing Department. "Being biracial is the best of both worlds! You've got two beautiful races in one package!" she'd tell me. According to my mother, a racial makeup like mine was a privilege bestowed only on a few special kids, like receiving a ten-speed bike or having a bedroom all to yourself. "As you get older, you'll see the benefits of being from two worlds," she said. In third grade, I discovered one of those benefits: getting out of the random head-lice checks by the school nurse.

I was a brand-new student in Sister Mary's third-grade class; a six-year-old public-school transfer in a room full of eight-year-olds. The head nun at my new Catholic school, St. Irenaeus, had decided that since I was already reading multisyllabic words, I could skip right over second grade.

For the first few weeks of class, I was extremely quiet, just trying not to mess up until I got the hang of the whole Catholic school routine. So the morning Sister Mary shouted, "Lice check! Everyone against the wall in size order!" I promptly shot out of my seat. When Sister Mary saw me trying to figure out my place in the size-order line, she pursed her lips as if to stifle a laugh and shook her head. "Not you, Angela," she called out, releasing her laugh.

Now, Sister Mary laughed only when one of her students did something unforgivably ridiculous, like forget how to spell *Irenaeus* or stammer over an apostle's name. She'd always cover her mouth after she laughed, as if she knew she shouldn't be so tickled by the dumbness of her students.

As I turned to sit back down, I noticed that my three black classmates, Eddie, Jackie, and Greg, had never even gotten up. How had they known to stay seated? *Does "everyone line up" mean only 100-percent-white children?* My mother was right. Catholic school was more challenging than public school.

While the majority of the class filed out, Sister Mary told us four remaining children to get a head start on our art project: drawing self-portraits. When Sister gave me a blank piece of paper, she said, "All God's children have their gifts. Black children are blessed. They don't get head lice."

I was too afraid to remind Sister Mary that my father was white; besides, she'd met him the first day of class. Although I wanted to question her choice in keeping me from having a scalp inspection, I'd learned during my brief time in her classroom that it was okay for Sister to question me, but I was never to ask *her* a question unless it had something to do with schoolwork or Jesus. Even then I had to be careful.

Two days earlier, Jimmy Callahan had gotten in trouble for questioning her about Jesus. Sister was standing over his head with red plastic art scissors, preparing to cut half his mullet off. Jimmy protectively clutched his long hair in his fists and screamed out, "This isn't fair! Didn't Jesus have long hair?"

"I'm married to Jesus!" Sister yelled, fingering the crucifix hanging from her neck. "Do you want me to tell him how bad you're acting?" That freaked me out. I couldn't concentrate the rest of the day. I didn't understand how she could be married to a dead man and wanted to ask her more about the particulars of that marriage, like did she actually have his body in her house or just his ashes, like my friend Karen had of her grandfather? How did she feel about people eating the body of her husband on Sunday? I kept my mouth shut because I didn't want her to yell at me or advise her husband to send me to Hell. I told my mother about the marriage and Sister Mary's yelling and crucifix-grabbing, but she dismissed the behavior as "obviously menopausal."

I crayoned accessories onto my self-portrait and decided to ask my mother if half-white kids could get head lice. If Sister Mary was wrong, this would be the second time my mother had corrected her. The first time, she'd corrected her covertly, acknowledging to me that I was right but refusing my plea to write a note telling Sister Mary so.

"Angela, I am not writing a note about chitlins to Sister Mary," my mother said. "But you were right; she probably never ate them."

I knew I was right. Sister Mary had sworn I was wrong, though. She embarrassed me in front of the entire class.

The chitlin incident happened during American history while we were going over the three pages in our book dedicated to slavery. We always read history lessons out loud, going up and down the aisles, with every student getting a paragraph. I always skipped ahead to see what paragraph we'd be on by the time we got to my desk.

To me, the only thing better than getting a nice long paragraph to read was having a surprise spelling bee. I might have been the youngest and got my ass beat regularly in kickball games, but I could outspell and outread everyone. My slavery paragraph was fat, full of commas and periods. I couldn't wait to dazzle the room with my perfect enunciation.

When my turn came, I dove into the words, reading them with

the zest and energy of a weathercaster. "The slaves made meals from the leftovers of their masters!" I said, making sure the tone of my voice reflected how horrific that was. "Some of the food slaves ate included pig's feet, chitlins, and—"

"Angela Nissel, please repeat that last word again," Sister Mary interrupted from the front of the classroom.

I looked down at the page, my eyes desperately scanning the word, trying to figure out if I'd skipped a letter or missed a vowel sound. Nope. I knew *chitterlings* was pronounced *chitlins* the same as *plough* looked like *rough* but was pronounced an entirely different way. My grandmother made chitlins once a month, and even though the bucket they came in sometimes said *chitterlings* everyone in the family said *chitlins*.

"Chitlins," I repeated loudly, thinking Sister Mary had misheard me.

Sister Mary laughed her quick laugh, then tightened her little lips into a frown and covered it with her palm. "It's chit-ter-lings, Angela. Break it into syllables."

I glanced up from my book and saw the whole class turned in their chairs, staring at me. I gripped my history book so tightly, the brown paper bag book cover had sweaty little fingerprints on it. I knew she didn't really expect me to sound out the word like a little kid, did she?

"Chit!" Sister Mary yelled, then looked at me expectantly.

"Chit," I repeated softly, eyes down, focusing on the smiling slaves in my book, wondering if they were happy because their masters didn't allow them to read, so they didn't have to go through humiliation like this.

"Ter!" Sister barked.

"Ter," I replied, a little louder.

Every white eye in the classroom looked at me, ready to giggle if I took another pronunciation misstep. I was getting the same looks Joey Shalaci got when he took twenty minutes to stutter through a sentence. The black kids' faces looked more serious; their eyes pleaded with me to hurry it along. Slavery was embarrassing. According to our American history book, it was black people's only contribution to this country. Here I was stretching it into syllables.

"Lings!" Sister Mary shouted, like she was giving a dog a command.

I sang the end back to her and exhaled, glad to be done with the torture.

"Now, put it all together," Sister Mary said.

"Chit-ter-lings," I said, my face about as pink as the pig's on the page. My mouth felt funny pronouncing *chitlins* like that. I knew Sister Mary was wrong. Unless she ate chitlins, how was she going to tell me how to pronounce them?

Before I could start to read the rest of my "what slaves ate" paragraph, Sister Mary interrupted again. "Does anyone know what chit-ter-lings are?"

Silence. Sister Mary looked around the room and frowned, like she suspected some people in the room were withholding information.

"Chit-ter-lings are pig intestines," Sister Mary explained. The entire classroom groaned, and some of the boys made dry heaving sounds. Sister Mary ignored the outburst and moved her gaze to the three brownest faces in the room. "Eddie, Jackie, Greg, do any of you eat chit-ter-lings?" Sister asked with a raised eyebrow.

Jackie shook her head *no*, so fearfully you'd have thought Sister was offering her a chance to be an actual slave. Greg, who was usually quiet, yelled, "Yuck! No!" Eddie didn't say anything; he simply dropped his head down on his desk as if he were dead.

"Eddie George, does your family eat chit-ter-lings?" Sister prodded.

If anyone in the class ate pig intestines, it had to be Eddie. He was known as the troublemaker. I don't know what he did to piss Sister Mary off so much, but she seemed to enjoy singling him out. I always wondered if her treatment of him scarred him for life, until I saw on the news that he went on to win the Heisman trophy and play for the Tennessee Titans. I saw him in a restaurant once and wanted to go over and ask if he remembered Chitlins Day, but I was afraid he'd think I was a football groupie with a really bad pro-black come-on line.

"I don't eat chit-ter-lings," Eddie replied, making his pronunciation perfect to avoid Sister's wrath.

Seemingly satisfied with his answer, Sister Mary looked at me. "Angela, do you or your mother eat chit-ter-lings?"

"No!" I lied. I was too young to understand the word *sellout* or know that if I got older and denied eating soul food to be accepted by white people, some people would revoke my black pass for life. In that moment, there was no way I was going to be the new six-year-old Methodist girl who ate pig guts. Sister Mary's husband would have to forgive me.

Sister Mary accepted my answer. I went on to read the rest of the paragraph perfectly, and the Third Grade Chitlin Inquisition was over.

The head-lice check was the second time I was grouped with Eddie, Jackie, and Greg but, unlike eating chitlins, not having head lice could be seen as a positive. I thought, Maybe all this race stuff evens out. For every embarrassing *chitterlings* experience, the kids with one or two black parents got a reprieve from something else embarrassing, like lice checks.

Still, as boring as going on a group excursion to the school nurse was, I felt awkward being one of only four students left behind. I wanted to be with the majority for once in this new school. It was bad enough that almost everyone else in my class was preparing for First Communion, a class I had to sit out of. I wanted to know so badly what communion tasted like. Was it a cookie or was it more like a wafer? I hoped it was a cookie, since my mother rarely let me eat high-sugar foods.

I drew one more pair of earrings on my self-portrait and started drawing in the background of my two-dimensional head. I drew my ideal bedroom, complete with two Menudo posters, even though I'd never listened to any of their songs. The popular girls at St. Ireneaus loved Menudo, so I figured maybe when they came back from the lice checks, they'd see my Menudo posters and let me walk home with them.

One by one my classmates started returning. As soon as a student showed Sister Mary his clean bill of head health, she had him start on his self-portrait. The returning and drawing flow was interrupted only when Joey Shalaci came back with his head down, holding up a bright pink note for Sister Mary. Sister Mary backed away from him and pulled a trash bag from the broom closet. She passed it down the aisle until it reached Joey, who stuffed all his belongings into it and exited. Everyone stopped drawing, and whispers buzzed around the room about Joey's failed head inspection.

"I guess since everyone is so talkative, everyone is done with their self-portraits," Sister Mary said, without looking up from her desk.

Always the A student, I raised my hand so I wouldn't be grouped with the talkers. "I'm done, Sister," I called out.

Sister Mary looked up at me in disbelief, like I was inconveniencing her by finishing so quickly. She propped both of her chubby hands up on her desk to help lift her sturdy frame from her chair, grabbed her beat-up cigar box of crayons, and slowly walked down my row.

She loomed silently over my desk for a second. I tensed up, wondering what mistake I had made this time. Would she make fun of my Menudo posters? Should I have drawn a crucifix instead?

"Angela, you should color in your face," Sister Mary said, rummaging through her cigar box, looking at various tan-hued crayons, and then squinting as she pressed them against my cheek.

First Joey had head cooties and now I had to color in my face? Way too much commotion in the classroom for one day. Giggles erupted from every desk. Well, almost every desk. The black kids stayed silent, of course. If she wanted light old me to color in my face, she might just suggest that we all just take turns using our Ash Wednesday leftovers to color in their faces.

Finally, Sister Mary found a crayon she thought best suited my complexion. "Here, Burnt Umber looks to be about right. Color your face in, and then you'll be done." Sister Mary held out a crayon that looked like it had never been used. Hot Magenta was worn down to a nub the size of a peanut, but in all the years this box existed, no one had even colored a shirt Burnt Umber.

I took the crayon, wishing it were a magic wand that could turn me into an ostrich so I could stick my whole head into sand until the school day was over. I'd remove my head only when I got home to ask my mother why I wasn't gray like an ostrich, because don't black and white combine to make gray? They certainly do not make burnt umber.

I decided I would rebel against face painting and started to color my hair with burnt umber. If Sister Mary asked, I'd tell her I couldn't get to my face; I had way too much hair. As I was coloring in the top of my left braid, Sister Mary called out to Jackie, Greg, and Eddie, "You three can come up to get crayons to make your faces darker too, if you want."

Of course they didn't want to. Didn't Sister Mary get it? We just wanted to fit in.

Tommy "Blimp" McCallum sat next to me, so I looked at his picture. Despite his nickname, he'd drawn himself thin as a rail. I wondered why Sister didn't suggest that Tommy draw himself with a double chin. Would it be wrong for me to raise my hand and suggest that? Tommy—like me, Jackie, Eddie, and Greg—drew himself as he *wished* he looked—as close to the majority and the popular kids as possible.

When we finished our drawings and broke for recess, I ran over to Karen and Kelly. They were the unpopular white girls (they didn't have perms) and the only friends I'd made so far. They knew how embarrassed I was. They knew what it felt like to have Sister Mary make a spectacle of you, so they did what all compassionate friends do, teased me about it in hopes I'd start laughing.

"Angela, color yourself in!" Karen said, mocking Sister Mary's voice.

I rolled my eyes and looked down. I wasn't ready to laugh yet.

Sister Mary was wrong about chitlins and she was wrong about my complexion.

"She's so mean," I said, hoping to steer the conversation to something else mean Sister did.

"Did you color yourself in?" Karen asked.

"No!" I exclaimed, as if even the thought of coloring my face in disgusted me.

"Well, you're almost the same color as us," Kelly said, and held her arm out next to mine. Karen held her arm out, too. My arm was darker, but not by much.

I flipped my hand so my palm faced the sky.

"On this side of our hands we're the same color," I said.

"Maybe this is your white side!" Karen exclaimed, pressing her palm against mine. I smiled politely at my new friend's observation, even though I knew that wasn't how the whole mixing-races thing worked. I was happy for the moment just to be accepted.

Mulatto Pride Turbo Boost

When it came to getting new electronics, my father was the consumerism king of the block. Every Saturday morning, he would brag to our next door neighbor about his latest acquisition while they were washing their cars. "Yeah, I just picked up this remote control that—hold on to your hat—isn't attached by a long cord to the TV." The next thing you know, people were pouring out of their row houses to test out our new devices. For a week after we got a refrigerator that dispensed ice and water straight from the door, people came by with big Slurpee cups, filling up and praising our appliance.

"This sure is something. How much a thing like this run?" our neighbor Mr. Glen asked, not paying attention as the water overflowed from his cup onto the floor.

"It's magic! A magic ice machine!" a woman we barely knew exclaimed, pressing for more ice and then giggling as it hit the bottom of her cup.

My father's latest purchase was a VCR that loaded from the top and churned as loudly as a food processor while rewinding. This VCR cemented our status as the most technologically advanced family on the block, and it provided me with a new way to overdose on my favorite activity—watching television.

When my parents started giving me an allowance for doing my chores, I negotiated for a 25 percent pay cut in order to extend my bedtime so I could watch *Knight Rider* and *Gimme a Break*. On school days, my mother would have to blast "Sexual Healing" by Marvin Gaye on my Fisher-Price record player to wake me up, but Saturday morning I'd be in front of the television at 7:30 A.M. sharp to catch up with my cartoons. My week would be ruined if I missed *Smurfs*. I didn't just watch them, I studied them. I could have written my third-grade dissertation on the closed market economy of the Smurf Village. I would pretend I was Smurfette and would frustrate my parents by refusing to improve my adjective vocabulary; to me, everything was "smurfy."

The smurfiest event of my childhood became my weekly trips to the video store with my father. Sometimes, if I'd gotten spanked during the week, my guilt-ridden father would salve my sore behind with an extra video store trip. In the middle of a whupping that barely hurt, I'd think, *If I cry really loud like I'm dying, I'll get to rent a Woody Woodpecker tape.*

Video Tape Library was a small store in our local strip mall. My father would let my brother and me pick out a cartoon tape while he looked at the new arrivals. I had just picked out my *Heckle and Jeckle* tape when Dad called out that it was time to go. I grabbed J.R.'s hand and followed him to the counter, where we stood by my father and waited for him to pay. The cashier suddenly stopped ringing up the videos and glanced down quizzically at my brother and me, then up to my father. "Do you know whose kids these are?" the cashier asked.

"Never seen them in my life," my father said, his eyes scanning our bodies, like if he concentrated hard enough he might figure out how these two kids got by his side.

Maybe Dad's gone crazy or has amnesia, I thought. Did he hit himself in the head recently? On the very cartoon tapes we rented from this place, I'd seen how, when characters fell off ladders, stars would orbit around their heads and they couldn't remember their own names. I tried to think whether my father had fallen recently or if I'd seen stars around his head. My brother probably didn't think anything. He was only two and the only word he had mastered was "bye-bye."

The cashier leaned over the counter so he could be at my eye level.

"Where are your parents?" he asked.

Hello, I'm a kid; probably the guy I'm standing next to and the guy my brother looks like a tan version of—that would be a parent. Of course, I didn't say that; I couldn't figure out what to do. My mind was overloaded by my father's denial of me. If your father denies you, should you deny him, too? The cashier is a stranger so I'm not allowed to speak to him without a trusted adult around but since my father has denied ever seeing me, technically he's no longer a trusted adult. I looked up at my father and tried to send him a telepathic message: *Come back, Dad. Think really hard. You do remember me.* He met my gaze with a blank look, so I stayed silent and stared at the cashier.

By this time, the cashier had to have been thinking, Great, I've not only got two lost black kids, they're also deaf-mutes. He tried a new tactic: rewording the question and speaking in the exaggeratedly loud, slow voice normally reserved for people who don't understand English.

"Who did you come to the vid-ee-o store with?" he yelled, his frustration mounting.

My father looked down at me like he was expecting an answer as well. I refused to speak to either of them.

With an expression that in my advanced age I now recognize as the *I don't get paid enough for this shit* look, the cashier stood back up and addressed the entire shopping audience.

"Whose kids are these?" he yelled. Everyone in the small video store glanced pitifully at the two lost black kids, shrugged their shoulders, and went back to perusing the tape selections.

I swear, incidents like this from my childhood are why I hate being stared at to this day. I'm so self-conscious, I leave home only when the line of cars on my street starts moving through the green light. If I leave on the red, people have nothing to entertain themselves with until the light changes, so they stare at me. I hate it. It makes me late for work.

With all corners of the store eyeballing me, I thought the next step would be some strange family snatching me up, claiming I belonged to them. The terror of losing my mother and my poodle kicked in. I yelled "Dad!" and yanked his T-shirt.

My father laughed. "These are my kids, man." The cashier looked at him for a moment, to ascertain if he was joking, and then lowered his head.

"I'm sorry. I thought, because they were . . ." The cashier's voice trailed off and he started ringing up our tapes. He gave the bar codes the same rapt attention I've seen anthropology professors give to rare caveman skulls, and handed our rentals over to us without a further word.

That was my last trip to Video Tape Library. I never wanted to go back after that. My father asked why I had suddenly lost interest in renting movies. Didn't I know *The Muppet Movie* had just been released? I wasn't sure how to explain my embarrassment to him, and I also felt I had let my parents down. I knew from my mother's lectures that I was supposed to be proud to be mixed, but the video store cashier had embarrassed me and I preferred to give up my hobby rather than ever feel like that again. I lied to my father and told him that VHS was out and I was interested only in Betamax movies, as that's the type of VCR the other parents on our block had started buying.

I had to find a new way to quench my craving for the programming that video tapes had previously provided. Because of those tapes, I hadn't had to suffer through reruns in over a year, and the thought of having to watch a show where I already knew the ending felt like punishment. I decided to explore other channels; to see what else was on when I got home from school.

I flipped the dial to a talk show. Even though I was catching up to the topic in the middle of the program, I quickly gathered that everyone in the studio audience agreed I should never have been born.

You couldn't turn on *Phil Donahue* in those days without seeing something about interracial couples. Invariably, the topic turned to What if the couples decided to have sex (the horror!) and gave birth to flawed, confused-race children? While people were generally in agreement that a grown man and woman could marry whomever they wished, the moment would come when a studio audience member would snatch the host's microphone, almost inhaling it before shouting, "Do you think it's fair to bring kids into the world who won't know who they are? What about the kids?" The studio audience would hoot and clap enthusiastically while Donahue smiled at them and said, "And we'll be back!"

I waited for them to come back. I was certain that when the commercials ended, I would see someone on the show who looked like me. A mixed-race kid, sticking up for all of us, telling everyone how beautiful and special we were.

That person never came out. I started realizing that no one on television looked like me. Not too many people were my mother's color, but at least she had a few representations—two and a half by my count: Nell Carter, Tootie, and the chunky mammy character from *Tom and Jerry* (the half point, since they only showed her calves). As stereotypical as they were, at least she had them. I started doubting my mother's stories about biracial children being beautiful and special. I began to suspect that my brother and I were the only mixed kids alive. I plotted to sneak up on my mother at an unexpected moment to see if she'd break down and confirm my suspicion.

"Mom, where are all the other mixed kids?" I asked while she was watching the news. She didn't like being interrupted when the Action News Team was on. My mother and her friends watched that newscast like they were being graded on it the next day. They all dressed their children according to the predictions of Dave Roberts, the quirky weatherman. If someone was caught in a hurricane without an umbrella, there was no pity, just admonishment. "Didn't you listen to Dave last night?"

Dave was king and the female news anchor, Lisa Thomas-

Laury, was queen. The adults talked about her reports as though she called the news straight to their phones instead of delivering it to two million Philadelphians simultaneously through the television. "Yeah, Lisa Thomas-Laury said the buses are going on strike," I heard my mother tell my father. Adult women carefully enunciated all three of Lisa Thomas-Laury's names, never disrespecting her by referring to her casually as Lisa.

"Lots of people are mixed," my mother said, looking at the ceiling as if she kept the mixed people's names written up there. "Like . . . uh . . . Lisa Thomas-Laury."

"She has green eyes!" I said. "She's white!"

"Who said mixed and black people can't have green eyes?" my mother replied. "My father has blue eyes." She was right; her father did have blue eyes. It wasn't until I was much older that I realized everyone with cataracts had the same cloudy blue eyes.

After that day, I became Lisa Thomas-Laury's youngest devotee. I would gladly sit through the whole newscast to see the only other mixed person I knew. I summoned the courage to ask my mother to help me mail her a letter. We decided on a postcard, since a prestigious woman like Lisa Thomas-Laury was probably too busy to open mail. I went with a simple greeting. *Hi, Mrs. Lisa Thomas-Laury. I'm mixed, too! Write back!*

She never wrote back. That could have been because, as I would later find out, she was not mixed and probably had no idea what the hell my postcard meant.

Back then, I didn't know my mother would lie to encourage self-love. In my mind, Lisa Thomas-Laury's lack of response meant she'd received my postcard, read it, and immediately trashed it. During school, I would daydream about the possible ways she had rid herself of my unwanted postcard—I had a full-blown panic attack during religion class after I fantasized about Ms. Thomas-Laury ripping my note up then tossing it under her car's tires for traction in a snowstorm. Watching her newscasts became painful; I was certain that she was just waiting for the right moment to annouce on air how she felt about my postcard.

"That's some bad weather, Dave. Speaking of bad, I received the most stupid fan letter recently...."

My mother soon realized I was spiraling into a depression whenever the news came on. She knew what she had to do—lie about another celebrity.

"David Hasselhoff is half black and half white," my mother mentioned casually after I collapsed into a crying spell while watching Lisa Thomas-Laury host the Thanksgiving Parade.

"Look at his skin! It's as tan as yours. And his hair," my mother continued. "Isn't that what your hair looks like when it rains?"

She was right. Michael Knight did have a curly 'fro! However, I still wasn't ready to risk the rejection of an unanswered fan letter, so I decided instead that my new idol would be the subject of my Black History Month oral presentation.

My new teacher, Sister Danielle, had given our class the assignment of independently researching an important black American to speak about. After sixteen consecutive oral reports on Martin Luther King, Sister Danielle expanded the topic criteria—we could also write about important people who were friends with black Americans.

The last day of February, I fidgeted in my seat as Emma Russell, the most popular girl in fourth grade, gave a stellar black history report on Abraham Lincoln. It was terrifying enough reading in front of the entire class without having to follow the Emancipation Proclamation done as a football cheer.

I took a deep breath before taking my place at the front of the classroom. I paced myself and held my head high as I rattled off two minutes and thirty seconds of David Hasselhoff trivia. Then I hit my last paragraph:

"Like me, David Hasselhoff has a German last name and a black mother."

Half the class burst into laughter. Rather than wait for them to settle down, I bit back tears and zoomed through the last sentences of my report.

"*KnightRider*isagreatshow. ItcomesonChannelsixateightP.M. Theend."

Sister Danielle asked if anyone had any questions for me. Tony Aiello, class bully, who was later expelled for breaking into the church and stealing a tape recorder, raised his hand.

"Knight Rider's not part black!" Tony called out.

"That's not a question, Tony," Sister Danielle snapped. "Phrase it as a question."

"Why would you lie and say Knight Rider is mixed?" Tony asked. His face turned bright purple, and his lips twisted like he wanted to curse me for sullying the sacred name of the premier nighttime television star.

"He's half black because my mother said he is," I replied.

We were still at the age where we respected our parents. Whatever they said was law, so Tony had no choice but to accept that I was right until he got home to ask his parents if my mother was wrong.

There were no further questions, so I walked back to my desk, mulatto pride fully intact.

"Good job! I learned a lot," Sister said, approaching me with her grading pen and giving me my first-ever A in public speaking.

As I gathered my papers, Sister leaned over and whispered in my ear. "Now, Knight Rider, that's the black fellow with all the gold chains and the mohawk, right?"

Zebra Kickball

"Zebras. You see, they're black, and they're white. The Black Panthers become the Zebras, and membership will double."

—*Sean Penn (as Samuel Bicke) in*
The Assassination of Richard Nixon

"Are you black or white?" Michael, a popular fourth-grade boy, asked me. We were around the corner from my house preparing to pick teams for a kickball game.

I knew I should have played with the black kids today, I thought as I glanced longingly down the street at the three black girls jumping rope. I wondered if it would be too obvious if I dashed away from the white kids and hopped into their rope.

It seemed the kickball game was on hold until I answered Michael, so I gave the response I'd been trained to give, the sentence that was as much a part of my childhood as knowing my phone number and the proper way to sit when wearing a skirt.

"My mom is black and my dad is white," I said.

"So you're a zebra!" Michael said. The kickball group gasped and giggled in amazement, like Michael was a comedic genius for calling someone who's mixed with black and white a zebra. If he were truly witty, he would have called me a panda or a penguin, I thought.

It was the first time I'd experienced opposition to my mother's standard-issue empowered-biracial-child answer. The word *just* in her instructions made it seem like a simple thing: *Just* tell them your dad is white and your mom is black; *just* answer honestly and then get back to playing kickball. I needed a sentence on what to do if an angry mob *just* didn't like that answer.

"Zebra!" another boy shouted, and the virus spread, infecting two more boys until there was only one boy not chanting the word. When that boy realized he was the only silent one, he sputtered out a half-hearted *zebra* under his breath and looked at me apologetically. I understood. No need for both of us to be misfits.

Michelle and Heather, two girls from my class, were laughing at the chant. The five boys, pleased with that bit of attention, decided that playing ring-around-the-zebra was more fun than kickball. "I am *not* a zebra!" I yelled as they circled around me. Unfortunately, no one could hear my great comeback over five male voices, so I expressed my anger by violently kicking their ball toward the sewer and then turned the other way and sprinted home.

Once inside the door, I tried to tell my parents what had happened but only one sound dropped out of my mouth. "Zee-zee-zee-eee," I said to my parents, trying to hold back my tears and talk at the same time.

My parents were actually smiling at me. Later, they admitted they thought I was imitating a deejay scratching a record, like in the rap songs that were beginning to get popular. Finally I spat it out. "Z-zebra! Zebra! They called me a zebra!" As the words flew out, so did my tears.

My mother shot my father a look, snatched me by one arm, and smushed my face into her overly powdered chest. I wheezed and cried while my father paced back and forth.

Once the last tear had flowed from my eye to her Jean Naté–flavored cleavage, my mother and dad went into the kitchen for a Grown Folks Meeting. Usually, when this happened, they'd mumble by the sink about how to punish me for some recent minor back-sassing. The last Grown Folks Meeting resulted in my not being able to watch TV for a week after I mimicked the sexy ways of a television circus trainer. "Why don't you come up and see me sometime?" I'd asked our mailman, and then licked my lips. This Grown Folks Meeting, it seemed, someone else was getting punished.

"I'm going to kill those little sons of bitches," my father said.

"And you'll go to jail!"

"*They* should be in jail!"

My father came out of the kitchen with my mother trailing him.

"Jack, where are you going?" she asked.

"To tell their parents. I won't hit anybody," my father said, grabbing my hand. "Show me where they live."

"I don't know where they live," I said, still swiping teardrops from my cheeks.

"We'll go to every door until we find them," my father assured me.

Suddenly, every tear was worth it. We were going door-to-door to kick some racist ass. It would be fun, just like trick-or-treating, except no candy and my father might punch someone in the face.

"Wait!" my mother yelled as we pushed through the screen door. I was afraid she was going to stop our mission, but she wanted only to wipe some of her bosom's baby powder off my nose. (That's my mother—how will you get people to stop teasing your daughter if you send her outside looking a mess?) Once she had wiped my face with a dab of saliva, it was time to go racist-boy-hunting.

My father didn't go door-to-door. Like the new microwave and electronic garage door he'd recently purchased, he was all about efficiency. My father saw Michelle and asked her where the boys lived. She squealed quickly, giving up the addresses of Michael, Teddy, and Jimmy, the three main chanters. My father thanked Michelle, and we stomped up Jimmy's front steps like his family owed us money.

After we rang the bell, a man and woman cautiously answered the door.

"Can I help you?" the man asked.

"Yes, you can," my father said. "Your son Jimmy called my daughter a zebra."

"Oh, God," Jimmy's mother said, slapping her palm to her forehead as if Jimmy always got into trouble and his antics were about to give her a nervous breakdown. She turned and shouted, "Jimmeee!" Jimmy came running down the stairs, stopping short of the last step when he saw me and my father.

"Did you call this girl a zebra?" Jimmy's father asked.

"Yeah, but I wasn't the only one—"

"I don't care who else did it. You apologize to her!" his father screamed, veins bulging from his neck.

"I'm sorry," Jimmy said, more to the carpet than to me.

"Are you okay with that?" my father asked me.

Are you okay with that? is one of those questions you shouldn't ask kids. Kids don't understand that some questions aren't meant to be answered truthfully. I didn't know I was supposed to say, *Yes, I'm okay with that.*

"No," I said, turning to Jimmy's father. "Is he going to get a beating?" I asked.

"Angela," my father said. In retrospect, I think he probably didn't want anyone to know he still doled out corporal punishment. Because of television news reports on time-outs being preferable to beatings, our family had switched from spankings administered by hand to ones given with a wet washcloth, as a sort of compromise. According to my mother, that method "packed all the sting and none of the marks."

"Yes, he is most certainly getting a beating," his mother replied. Jimmy started crying and flew back up the stairs. It's my only memory of taking pleasure in someone else's pain. It felt damn good. We could have quit going to houses right then, as far as I was concerned.

At Michael's house, the front door was open. Through the screen door, I could see Michael and his family eating in the kitchen. Before we could ring the doorbell, a short, thick-necked dog raced to the door and growled at us. Michael's father came soon after. He squinted at us and frowned.

My father started talking through the screen door. Michael's father lit a cigarette and drummed his fingers against the door frame, as if he was growing impatient with my father's interruption of his dinner. I smiled nervously at the dog and he started growling again.

"And your son was one of the boys who called her a zebra," my father said, ending his complaint.

"Who's that?" Michael's mother yelled from the kitchen.

"Nobody," Michael's father called back, without taking his eyes off my father. He then took a long puff from his cigarette, leaned past us, and flicked the smoldering butt into the street. Without a word, he shut the door in our faces. My father stared at the door and bit his lip as if contemplating something. After a moment, he turned down the steps to leave. As we hit the street, I smashed the smoldering cigarette with my shoe to make sure the fire was completely out.

We didn't go to Teddy's house. Instead, we headed home in silence. *Well, that last house sucked,* I wanted to say, but I wasn't allowed to use the word *sucked.*

My mother was waiting in the living room. "How'd it go?" she asked my father. He sped past her into the kitchen. I followed him.

"One man got really pissed at his son," my father yelled back to her, removing a small Ex-Lax package from a cabinet. He slammed the cabinet shut and took out some cheese from the refrigerator. He wrapped a chunk of cheese around an Ex-Lax pill. "The last guy was a jerk. And he owns the dog that's been pooping on our lawn," my dad continued.

My mother ran into the kitchen and grabbed the cheese from my father's hand. "Jack, it's not the dog's fault. Don't hurt the dog."

Dad's hurting a dog? With cheese? Does he have a cheese pellet gun in the toolshed?

"Dad, what are you doing to his dog?" I cried, worried that my zebra fight was going to result in a doggie death.

"He's putting something out for the dog to eat that will give him the poops," my mother said, trying to get me on her side, since I'd brought the battle home in the first place.

"Gwen, the man slammed the door in our face, and his dog craps in our yard! He's lucky this is all he's getting."

My parents were usually so straight and narrow, my mother especially, that I could have been a Brady kid. I couldn't watch R-rated movies or wear nail polish like my classmates. Once, when I tried to steal a pack of gum from Rite Aid, my mother caught me and made me apologize to the store manager. He looked embarrassed for me. It got tiring. Whenever I got the rare chance to witness them doing something devious—like the time my brother picked up a toy in a store and my mother, not seeing a price tag on it, exclaimed, "It's free!" and stuck it in her purse—I tried to make it last as long as I could.

"Will the poops hurt the dog?" I asked.

"No, just Michael's father's carpets," my father replied.

"Mom, we have to do it," I turned to her. I thought the plan was as full of holes as the cheese, like what if Michael's father let the dog out before the diarrhea started and the dog got diarrhea in our yard? What if a squirrel ate the Ex-Lax? Is it really revenge if it's done anonymously? Can we put a note on the dog's collar saying "Who's a zebra now?" It might not correlate exactly, but Michael's family would get the point.

My mother sighed. "Well, I do want that dog to stop pooping in our yard," she said, giving in. "Can you at least not use the good cheese? We do have some that's about to expire, you know." With that, she gave my father her blessing as well as a half-opened package of Velveeta.

My father gave me a fresh Ex-Lax tablet and showed me how to squeeze the cheese tightly around it. We walked hand in hand to our side yard to place it in the grass, our energy recharged. We were getting racial justice the American way, through revenge and the harming of innocent bystanders.

· · ·

The next morning, I lay in bed, howling and clutching my stomach, trying to convince my mother I had the flu. I was afraid I was going to get beaten up when I got to school. It was bad enough to get someone in trouble with the teacher, but the punishment for getting someone in trouble at home was even worse. God looked out for me that next day, though. There was a new student in my class, someone the boys decided it was even more fun to pick on. My new classmate, Sean, was "slow," according to Sister Mary. He certainly talked and read more slowly than the other students. He also ran more slowly, so he wasn't of any use to the boys at recess. Instead of handball, they teased him for the entire thirty minutes.

"Sean, say *fluorescent*," Michael commanded, his newest bullying game being to order Sean to say complicated words and time how long he took to say them. If Sean took more than four seconds to repeat a word, Michael would yell out, "Sean's stupid!" On the bus ride home, the girls whispered about Sean. "Sean's a 'tard!" they said. If they caught someone looking at him, they'd giggle. "You like the 'tard!"

I was so relieved that Sean's presence prevented any hassle I expected for taking my father to Michael's door, I ran home and yelled, "Mom! There's a new 'tard in my class!" Before I could get to the part of how I was grateful for the 'tard because everyone was so busy teasing him they forgot about me, my mother's face soured and she screamed, "Go to your room and don't come out until I tell you to!" I had no idea what I'd done wrong.

After an hour, my mother came upstairs and explained that 'tard was just as hurtful as *zebra*.

"The correct word is"—my mother's face strained—"the correct word is *retarded*," she said, forcing parental certainty into her voice.

The ironic nature of that moment didn't occur to me until I was much older. If my mother, a nurse who had definitely come in contact with mentally handicapped/differently-abled/retarded people wasn't sure of the 1983 politically correct way of referring to such people, how were the well-meaning parents in the formerly all-white neighborhood instructing their children to refer to me? After Jimmy got his beating for calling me a zebra, did his mother struggle through a diversity lesson? "Angela is not a zebra, she's black and white so the correct word is . . . uh . . . *blite.*"

There was no kickball around 72nd Street for the rest of the week; it seemed like everyone was on punishment for either a *zebra* or *'tard* comment. The only kids outside were Sean and Michael (and his diarrhea dog, who still fertilized our lawn daily). The weird thing is, that week that Michael and Sean were forced to play together, Michael became Sean's friend and guardian.

A few days after the memory of punishment had worn off, someone pushed Sean during kickball and called him a 'tard.

"He's not a 'tard!" Michael said, standing nose to nose with the offender until he mumbled an apology.

"Yeah, you better apologize, you fag," Jimmy said, returning to his spot in the kickball game.

Once You Go Half Black

"What's there to talk about?"

—Tom Cruise, responding to Oprah Winfrey's
asking if he's ever talked about race to his
biracial son

Whenever my mother called me *child,* **I knew I was tap**
dancing on her last nerve.

"Child, you really must not want Santa to come to our house
tomorrow!" my mother yelled after I ignored her *go to bed* for the
third time that night.

I had just turned eight and, like most other kids my age, I lived
in fear of people I didn't know (Santa Claus, the Tooth Fairy, the
Lord) and the things they would deny me if I misbehaved (presents, money, the pearly gates of heaven). I wasn't even certain I believed in Santa anymore, but I had more fear of offending the jolly
white stranger than I did my mother. I'd be damned if I was going
to risk getting coal in my stocking.

The next morning, I came downstairs and Santa was snoring on our sectional. It was the first time I gasped at the sight of
another human being.

"He got tired and stayed here for the night," my father explained, nudging Santa awake.

As Santa stood up, I noticed that he looked considerably skinnier than he did at Macy's. He grabbed a Hefty bag full of presents
from our coat closet and leaned in my face. "Have you been a good
girl this year?" he asked. His eyes were bloodshot and his breath

smelled hot and fruity, just like Mr. Ron's, my dad's alcoholic assistant.

"Mom, it's Mr. Ron!" I screamed, running behind her legs.

"Ho, ho, ho, no, I'm not!" Mr. Ron said, reaching behind my mother to pick me up, blasting me again with his Mad Dog breath.

"Angela, stop being silly! That's the real Santa!" my mother insisted.

"Seriously, Mom! That's Mr. Ron!" I lowered my voice. "You know—the drunk!"

My mother gasped as if she had never used the word to describe this man. My father widened his eyes in horror. "Go to your room, immediately!" he commanded. "Now J.R. will get all Santa's gifts and you'll get nothing," he went on as my brother walked down the stairs. My father grabbed my brother and plopped him into Mr. Ron's lap. Instead of going straight to my room, I lingered on the steps to watch the action.

My brother took one look into Santa's bloodshot eyes and started screaming and kicking. Santa tried to hold J.R. by the waist, but child fear must be stronger than adult muscle. My brother scratched at Mr. Ron's face and eventually pulled his strap-on beard clean off.

I couldn't resist screaming my righteousness from the steps. "I told you! It's Mr. Ron!"

"Child, didn't we tell you to go to your room?" my mother yelled. I scampered up the steps, mad as hell that I got in trouble for telling the truth.

I held on to that anger for months after Drunk Santa. I set out on a mission to disprove other illusions my parents had forced upon me. I stepped on every crack in the sidewalk ("Look, Mom, I didn't break your back!"); I threw a fit in Sears ("How come the security guard isn't arresting me, Mom? You said he'd handcuff me if I acted up"). She acquiesced that she had lied ("He might not arrest you, but I will whip your smart little behind if you don't stop!").

There was one illusion she seemed unwilling to give up. My

mother insisted that, regardless of color, people were all the same.

Even at eight years old I could see that evidence to the contrary was everywhere we turned, as plain as Mr. Ron dressed up as Santa. I had no hard data on the differences between black and white men, but I suspected the patterns echoed that of the women. Through visits to my all-white playmates' homes, I learned that white women smoked Virginia Slims, got perms, and headed to the Jersey Shore covered in tanning oil as soon as the weather went above 70 degrees.

Through trips to the all-black beauty salon with my mother, I learned that black women smoked Newports, got Jeri-Curls, and preferred to stay in someone's air-conditioned house when the weather got hot. The only reason to go to Jersey was if a friend had organized a bus trip to Atlantic City.

Those beauty salon visits also taught me not only that people were not equal in their daily habits but, actually, that people of different races should stay separated. Black people walking through white neighborhoods could lead to violence and food waste.

"Miss Jessie was on her way to church and them white boys threw eggs at her," Miss Lillian, the salon owner, said, applying a thick white paste to my mother's scalp.

My mother whipped her head around to look Miss Lillian in the eye to see if she was lying. All the children in the salon ducked as Jeri-Curl solution flew from my mother's head and splattered on the walls.

"White people are just born evil," another customer commented, without looking up from the pages of *Vogue* magazine. "I'm tired of this curl," she continued. "Can you make my hair bone-straight, like hers?" she asked, holding up a photo of Christie Brinkley.

Getting your hair done was a half-day affair. While my mother waited for her turn under the circular hair dryer, I'd play with Alicia, the salon owner's daughter.

"What would you do if white boys threw eggs at you?" Alicia asked me.

"Nobody is going to throw egg at me. My dad is white," I said, obviously too young to be up on the Aryan Nation's laws of racial purity. I was certain being half white was almost the same as being white. I knew I often endured some teasing that the white kids didn't—the zebra name-calling, taunts about my hair feeling like a Brillo pad—but where I used to get upset, now I hid my anger and chalked it all up as an initiation. I convinced myself that the teasing had to stop one day, and after that I would be welcomed into the fold as an honorary white person. As bad as the ridicule got at times, watching the three black girls on the block who were never invited to play with the white kids helped keep me from crying or running home and telling my parents every time someone started teasing me.

Jacqui, Kim, and Lisa always played on the sidewalk right in front of one another's houses, as if there were an invisible fence preventing them from going into the street or around the corner. When my white friends weren't outside—usually when they were at a party I wasn't invited to or went down to the Jersey Shore with their moms—I'd join the three black girls. Playing with them was the only time my two black Barbies came out of their motor home. (Who said black people don't like camping?)

I'd made the mistake of bringing a black Barbie out to play with the white girls once, but they treated her like dirt, like she was Scurvy Barbie.

"Ewww! That's not Barbie," Michelle said, backing her Western Barbie away. I agreed with Michelle, and not just because she was the queen of the pack. Anyone who watched television could tell Black Barbie wasn't as important as White Barbie. White Barbie dominated the commercials: She was the one cruising the coast in a Corvette; she was the one taking the elevator to the second floor of the Dream House. Black Barbie appeared only in a still shot behind White Barbie for about two seconds before the commercial faded to black.

With Michelle and the gang looking on to see how I would

handle. ousting Black Barbie, I had Skipper tell Black Barbie she couldn't play with the group, and then I threw her back into her motor home.

Soon after benching Black Barbie, I learned that black friends were also to be played with only in secret. Once, I walked to the schoolyard with Jacqui, the only black girl from my block who went to St. Irenaeus.

Jacqui usually sat on the steps alone, but this time I sat down with her. Michelle noticed us and motioned me over with her finger. "Why are you sitting there?" she asked, her voice full of irritation.

"Because I walked with her this morning."

"Don't play with her," Michelle said, offering no further explanation as she pulled me by the arm toward the group of white kids. "If you play with her, you can't play with us."

I walked away and left Jacqui sitting in the grass while the white kids played around her and almost through her, not even apologizing when a Nerf ball hit her on the head.

Back in the beauty salon, the same conversations that clued me in on the benefits of segregation also let me know that, despite what my mother said to me in private about people being equal, she knew it wasn't really the case. Once, she'd laughed with her friends as she recounted how she almost got into a fistfight with a woman over a Cabbage Patch doll.

"The white women wanted Cabbage Patch dolls so bad, they were even grabbing the black ones!"

I took that to mean that white women didn't usually want black dolls. Black dolls were somehow not as good as white ones.

That same day, Alicia was getting her first relaxer. Her mother, Miss Lillian, complained about the hassle of dealing with such a tumbleweed of hair every morning and used the same words to describe Alicia's hair as the white girls used to tease me about mine: bad, thick, nappy. After Alicia's mother put the chemicals on her hair, she undid one of my two braids and pulled her fingernails through the tight curls above the back of my neck.

"She should get a relaxer, too," Miss Lillian advised my mother. "She has some tough, thick hair back in this kitchen," she said, painfully pulling on my tangled curls.

"She has that good hair; it's probably too delicate for a perm," another customer replied.

"Yeah, I wouldn't put that in her hair," my mother agreed.

Alicia winced in pain and screamed for her mother to rinse the burning perm solution out of her hair. I was horrified but at the same time grateful that my half-white side saved me from being lumped with the black people. I became determined to use that side as an all-access pass to the world of real Barbies and pain-free hair for as long as I could.

Every two weeks as my mother got her hair curled, the stories of racial clashes became more violent. Black people who ventured into the wrong neighborhoods were getting egged, along with a side order of ass-kicking.

"Li'l Man said those white boys tried to stab him!" Miss Lillian announced.

"Miss Jessie is now carrying mace in her purse!" another woman added.

"I'm telling you, someone is really going to get hurt," Miss Lillian said.

"If I need to go through the white neighborhoods, I always wear my uniform," one lady said, fingering her U.S. Postal Service hat. "Them white boys don't mess with me. They know I won't deliver their mothers' welfare checks!"

"I've been through the sixties. No white boys are going to stop me from shopping!" my mother yelled from under the hair dryer.

And my mother meant it. I was terrified for her as she dragged me along to Talluto's, an Italian deli right on the corner of where Miss Lillian said a guy threw a pumpkin at her on Halloween. My mother had been faithful to Talluto's ever since my paternal grandmother died. Up until her death, my grandmother insisted I get to know my Sicilian roots and eat only the best pasta and pizza sauce.

Two days after some white teenagers firebombed an interracial couple's house on the same block as Talluto's, my mother still insisted on shopping there.

Every night, we saw Talluto's at the beginning of the evening as Channel Six started off the local newscast with colorful graphics and a play on fire words: Racial Tensions Heat Up!

"Mom, these people want to kill you!" I warned her when she was getting out of the car to buy pizza sauce.

"Angela, the police car is sitting right there," my mother said, and she pointed to a cruiser that was stationed at the end of the block to keep the peace. That made me even more jittery, but I got out of the car thinking I could protect my mother with my half-white powers if someone tried to set her on fire. Fortunately, I never had to test my powers out, but I often wonder what we looked like to other people. What did they think of the black mother pulling her child through a race-riot zone to buy pizza?

My mother wouldn't be contained by racial tensions, but the more they grew, the more she contained my play boundaries. I received a bike for my birthday, but it was more like a museum piece than a toy. I couldn't ride it more than two feet. The day my father took the training wheels off, my mother brought me onto the front porch and outlined my safe area. "Angela, your field of play is here and here," she said, circling our block and the block across the street with her finger. "You cannot go there, there, there, or there," she said, circling everywhere else.

Jacqui was watching as my mother reiterated my play boundaries. *I knew you'd be joining me again sooner or later,* her eyes seemed to say, as my mother drew another invisible **X** over the field of grass that separated our block from the all-white neighborhoods.

I still refused to join Jacqui and her friends—not after Michelle's threats of ousting me from the white group. I sat on my steps ignoring the black girls as my white friends cycled by, playing cards flapping from the spokes in their back wheels.

"Hey! Wanna play Barbies?" I called out to them as they zoomed past me, my feet firmly planted on the very edge of my mother's outlined boundaries. "Wouldn't it be fun to sit on my steps and play?" They ignored me.

Instead of playing outside, I spent the next few days in the mirror, analyzing what parts of my body I would have to change to be fully accepted by the white people. My lips should be a little bit smaller. I sucked them in. My nose should have more of a point, I thought, and pushed it together with my hands. I did get a little bit lighter from being inside so much, but it wasn't enough. My boundaries stayed the same.

I went back outside and decided that playing by myself was the best thing to do. I'd throw a Frisbee, chase it, and throw it again, laughing loudly enough for Jacqui to hear. *I don't need you; look at how much fun I'm having playing schizophrenic Frisbee! Ha ha ha!*

Finally, boredom set in, and it was just as strong as half-white pride. I slunk up to the black girls. Even after my multiple shameful refusals to play with them, I was warmly welcomed back into the fold and shown how many games one can play within ten feet of sidewalk space.

When we were tired of playing Chinese jump rope, marbles, Mother May I, and Red Light Green Light, we undid one another's braids. They also wore their hair parted down the middle, pulled into two thick braids, and secured with elastic. There was no teasing about hair, no mention of Brillo pads; we'd exchange barrettes as a sign of friendship.

After a few weeks, I learned Jacqui and her friends were scared of white people but curious about them as well. My background as an ex-friend of white kids made me the perfect conveyor of information.

"Are all white people's houses dirty?" Jacqui asked me.

I told them the truth, which seemed to shock them. "No, some white people's houses are clean," I said.

"Are you sure? My mother said white people are dirty," Kim asked.

"All white people do smell like wet dog, though," Jacqui stated. "Does your dad smell like wet dog?"

"No, that's crazy!" I said. No matter how comfortable I felt with them, I wasn't about to betray my white side wholly.

"You're lying. I want to come into your house after it rains and smell for myself!" Kim said.

I promised them they could come over during the next rainstorm. That next rainy day we gathered in my basement, practicing steps—the black version of cheerleading with no pom-poms and more rhyming words. We were excessively loud, and my mother and father came downstairs to see what we were doing. I jumped up to show my parents.

"My name is Angie and I am fine! I am fine, just like my sign! My sign is Sagittarius!" I yelled, rotating my hips like I was twirling a hula hoop. My mother clapped. My father walked out of the room.

"I don't want her learning street games!" my friends and I heard him yell from upstairs. I knew street games meant black games. My new friends were terrified; they froze, looking to me for guidance.

I hated my dad at that moment. I thought he was no different from the arson supporters on television. Looking back, I'm more forgiving. I know preconceived notions don't die because you marry someone of a different skin tone. I wonder if parents realize that, despite how much love you give your children, one word said in anger can change how they feel about you and themselves.

I sniffed the air. "Do you smell something?" I asked Jacqui. She shook her head *no*.

"I smell it," I said, sniffing the air and moving toward where my father's yelling could be heard more clearly. "It smells like wet dog," I said, hoping my face looked astonished.

Jacqui and Kim got up cautiously. "Wait, I think I smell it, too!" Jacqui said.

"I told you! It's your dad!" Kim whispered.

"My dad smells like Chihuahua!" I said, throwing out the funniest dog name I could think of. I inhaled deeply and pretended to pass out.

Jacqui and Kim fell to the floor, laughing.

I felt a pang of shame—how low can you go?—sniffing around my basement and selling out my father for a chance at friendship. The pang was easily snuffed by thinking of how angry I was at him and how much acceptance I would gain by selling him out.

Even the joy of acceptance came uneasily. I have always been a worrier (so much so that people constantly ask me if I'm sure I'm not Jewish). How much more of what my parents told me was really a lie? Why was stepping a street game and kickball wasn't? What would happen if Kim and Jacqui sniffed me one day and decided they smelled "half wet dog?" It seemed that race, like whether Santa Claus was real or not, was something I would have to figure out on my own.

Miss Julie

First marriages in which the husband and wife are members of the same race/ethnicity are more likely to succeed than those in which the spouses are of different race/ethnicity.

—Cohabitation, Marriage, Divorce and Remarriage in the United States, *National Center for Health Sciences, Vital Health Stat (23) 22, 2002*

Being a mixed child, you get used to people staring at you. I learned that rolling my eyes or sticking out my tongue was the quickest way to get people to avert their gazes. Even now, when someone stares at me—if the person doesn't look like the concealed-weapon type—I sometimes revert to my adolescent days, rolling my eyes and mumbling hollow threats under my breath: "If you don't stop staring at me . . ."

"You've really got to stop threatening old ladies," my husband says. I know, I know—but until they start a tragic-mulatto twelve-step group, I'm doing the best I can.

My mother, a bigger fan than I of the *kill them with kindness* approach, used to start conversations with the starers. "Hello!" she'd say, in an overly cheery voice. Usually the person would reply with an awkward smile or simply continue staring, mouth agape, as if they were startled that a woman with a half-white child could speak English.

I remember a few black women coming right out and asking if my father was white. The white women never did that; they said nothing with their lips; their eyes would say it all: *How in the world did that happen?* Our family vacation photo album actually has a section called Staring White Women. Every time we got pictures developed, my mother noticed a few in which she'd be posing with me while in the background a white woman stares at us, eyes squinting as if she's unsure of what she's looking at. My favorite photo in that collection is from Disney World. As my multiracial family cheeses in front of the Haunted Mansion, in the background you can see Snow White gawking at us, ignoring the screaming children at her feet.

Before I learned to stick out my tongue, the staring would make me uncomfortable. I hated walking to school alone in first grade; the crossing guard used to drill holes into me with her eyes. One day we'd had a police officer come to our class to teach us about kidnappers. I became convinced that the crossing guard was trying to kidnap me. I told my mother of this fear in the beauty parlor.

"No one kidnaps black kids," her hairdresser replied.

"If they do, they bring them right back," another woman said, laughing.

On the last day of school, my mother walked me to school, and finally the crossing guard spoke.

"You're so pretty," she said, leaning in closer. "Is your father white?" When I replied *yes,* she reached into her pocket and gave me a piece of hard candy. "Here's a present for my cute little mulatto," she said, showing all her teeth.

"Don't eat that candy," my mother whispered. I ate it anyway. I had no clue that my mother was afraid the crossing guard was a racist who carried a pocket full of poisoned candies just in case she encountered someone like me.

"Mom, the cashier is staring at me," I said as my mother gathered her purse to go pay for a fill-up on pump seven.

"She's staring because you're so pretty," she said, and left my brother and me in the car as she approached the cashier's booth and slid five dollars into the drawer. Instead of taking my mother's money, the cashier kept staring at me. My mother tapped on the bulletproof glass. The cashier leaned into the microphone, and instead of your normal gas station cashier-customer chitchat ("What pump are you on?" or "We're all out of Newports"), the cashier screamed out my name.

"Angela! I'd recognize your little high-yellow butt anywhere!" The confused look on my face led her to continue. "I saw your picture, the one with you holding the Read-A-Thon trophy! I'm good friends with your dad, sweetie!"

Oh, God, why do I have to look so different from everyone, so recognizable? I put the blame on my complexion instead of where it belonged: *Why doesn't my father take down my photos when he's sexing a mistress in the house?*

My mother rapped on the glass again, this time like she was trying to shatter it. This caused the cashier to realize she was shouting *too much information* through a gas station mike. She unlatched the door to her tiny booth, and my mother walked in. After a few moments of making sure their conversation wasn't turning into a cage match, I grabbed my brother's hand, got him out of the car with me, and squeezed us both into the booth next to my mother.

"Angela, this is Miss Julie," my mother said, like she was introducing me to British royalty. She was using her high-pitched things-aren't-okay-but-I'm-damned-sure-going-to-pretend-they-are voice. She didn't have to front; I already knew my parents were having problems and she suspected my father was cheating. (Note to parents: Trying to have cryptic conversations by spelling words out no longer works once your child is reading.) I hadn't come into the booth to hear about the cheating. I had two things on my mind. One, I wanted to ask Miss Julie what "high yellow" meant. (*Zebra, mulatto, mixed, high yellow—so many words to learn to call myself, so little time.*) Two, I wanted my mother back.

Ever since the first argument about my father c-h-e-a-t-i-n-g with w-h-o-r-e-s, my mother had started working a lot: double shifts, triples, the graveyard shift. (Some people drink to escape their problems; my mother works. It was an addiction that worked out well financially for the family, since my dad worked only sporadically.) I rarely got to see my mother. Miss Julie was sucking up my precious moments.

"I ain't never seen a black woman come up here with half-white kids. Hell, I ain't never been in a white man's house where he got half-black kids on the walls and shit," Miss Julie said. "This here done fucked up my high. For real."

Suddenly, I wasn't in such a rush to get out of the booth. I'd never heard anyone admit to doing drugs or curse so much—and so well. Miss Julie was taking curse words I knew and merging them with other curse words, thereby creating wonderful new double-layered curse words ("Yeah, he must have thought I was some bitch-ass trick"). She was using curse nouns as verbs ("Your husband asked me for free gas, but I'm, like, motherfuck that"). I sat down in Miss Julie's chair. For this, I could share my mother.

"You know, when a regular black guy comes up and starts hitting on you, it ain't nothing new, but when it's a white man, you start feeling all special and shit. I thought he had some money. I didn't know he was a broke ass."

My mother looked cautiously at me, torn between wanting to know more and shielding my head from the flurry of swear words raining down on it. I pretended I wasn't listening. I swiveled on Miss Julie's chair, watching the cars pulling up.

"You and your daughter look just the hell alike, except she's light. Now, your son, he has some color. How'd that shit happen?"

How *did* that shit happen? I didn't have time to contemplate it. My mother ripped two packages of Reese's Pieces off the display rack and stuffed them in my hands. "Here, feed some to your brother."

"Yeah, I met him right here," Miss Julie continued. "He came up to the window asking can he get free gas. Free gas, my ass," Miss

Julie said, rolling her eyes. She talked for ten minutes without one interruption from my mother. She didn't even break her verbal stride when customers approached. I marveled at her multitasking; she was taking money for gas, pushing numbers in on the cash register, while detailing to my mother the times she'd been in our home. I don't know why she was so excited to give up this information; perhaps my dad cheated on her as well. "He said he was going to give me that rocking chair you got in your bedroom. I never got the shit—"

"I want to go to Chuck E. Cheese," my brother yelled, pulling on my mother's shirt.

Before my mother could answer, Miss Julie leaned over me and showed him how to push the drawer out to get people's gas money. My brother, who could be content for hours with just a cardboard box, fell in love with the money drawer. Chuck E. Cheese left his mind. "You want to talk on the microphone, sweetie?" Miss Julie asked me, lowering it to my height. When people came up to the booth, instead of talking to them, she delivered the responses through me while still holding court with my mother. "Angie, tell him we don't have no more menthols. . . . Gwen, yeah, I did end up giving him five dollars of free gas. . . . Angie, tell him pump number five is broken, honey. . . . Gwen, who did the tiles in your bathroom? I like the pink and white thing." My mother kept giving me more candy every time I finished a package.

I was preoccupied with doing well at my new job. Within minutes, I knew the difference between 100s and regular cigarettes and what color tree air freshener went with what scent. Then I heard something that meant our time in the gas station booth was going to be over soon: two uses of the F word in one sentence ("So I'm, like, 'Fuck him'; I'm not fuckin' getting fired for his ass").

Awww, man, I thought. If Miss Julie keeps it up, we're going to have to leave. My mother tolerated cursing around kids only in extreme circumstances, but her patience wore thin at multiple F bombs. I'd lost friends over that word. One time, I was over at

Shelly's house, and her mother and dad got into an argument. Shelly's mother yelled at her father, "I give you fucking blowjobs and you do *this*?" I went home and asked my mother what a *fucking blowjob* was. She covered her mouth as if she'd seen a ghost; then she exclaimed, "Well, I'll be a monkey's uncle!" I was never allowed to play at Shelly's again.

Miss Julie could talk about my father's penis, smoke, stare, and call me "high yellow," but once she said *fuck* two times in one sentence again, it was time to go.

"Well, we have to get to the store," my mother said finally, got Miss Julie's number (she already had ours), and piled us into the car.

We rode in silence for a few minutes. I knew the silence meant she was upset, so I tried to make mother-daughter small talk.

"Mom, what's high yellow?"

"Nothing. Don't worry about it," she said, looking straight ahead.

I tried again. "Mom, I want to work at a gas station when I grow up."

"No, you don't," she said, still staring straight ahead even though we were at a stoplight. Right before the light turned green, she added, "Don't tell your father who we met."

I was mad that our day together wasn't turning out to be *our* day at all.

"Free gas, my ass!" I mumbled, imitating Miss Julie and knowing that a curse would irritate my mother.

My mother pulled the car right over. This time she looked at me. "If I ever hear you curse again, you're getting a spanking. When we get home, you go straight up to your room."

I was pissed. "Ass is not a curse! It's a donkey! It's not a curse!" I lied like I believed my lie.

"Child, don't give me any lip! When we get home, go right upstairs, pack a bag, and put it under your bed. We're going on a trip soon," my mother said, turning the radio on.

This time, I was the one who stayed silent. I was steaming. It would be so much more fun to have Miss Julie as a mother. We could curse and eat candy all day. I could ask her what high yellow meant. Why couldn't my mother be more like Miss Julie? I wondered.

"You are in so much trouble, young lady," my mother reminded me, as we pulled up to our door.

The only consolation I had was knowing that my dad was in way *more* trouble. As I started packing my book bag full of clothes, I had a feeling he was not going to be invited on our impromptu trip.

Inner City Stars

In a culture that idealizes whiteness and deval-
ues blackness, black children frequently identify
with the white dominant race. With the interracial person being half white and therefore
closer to a white Euro-American frame of reference and privileges than uniracial blacks, becoming black is even more of a challenge.

—*Ursula M. Brown*, The Interracial
Experience: Growing Up Black/White
Racially Mixed in the United States

Nana, my maternal grandmother, was a hard, round
woman who used to dry my mother's hair by sticking her head in
the oven. I knew this because whenever I would complain about
how long it took my hair to dry, my mother would remind me that
it was better than having to hold your head still next to a pot roast.

"Your nana loves *in her own way*," my mother would say. I knew
that was the adult way of calling someone mean. At Nana's house,
there was no running and no loud talking, and questioning adults
was considered back talk, something punishable by beatings with
a switch. When my mother told me and my brother that we were
moving there until she could save up enough money to get our
own place, I sat shotgun in our Ford Granada, desperately trying
to think of other alternatives.

"Can we live in the library?" I asked.

"Are you still scared that Nana is going to bake your braids off?" my mother asked. "Nana stopped using the oven years ago. She has a microwave now; it dries hair quicker."

I wasn't in a joking mood. I stroked my plaits like they were puppies.

My mother sighed. "Don't tell your grandmother I told you about that. She didn't know putting my head in the oven was dangerous. . . ." Her voice trailed off like there was more to say but she decided against it, or maybe the effects of inhaling stove gas on shampoo days were kicking in on my mother's brain at that very moment.

I decided to give my nana the benefit of the doubt on the oven story. It's possible that she didn't know you could die from sticking your head in an oven; she talked about her lack of formal education the same way some people always find a way to toss out that they graduated second in their college class. If you hung around my grandmother for five minutes, you'd know she was Sylvia Smith, SGC (Sixth Grade Completer).

"What do I know? I only went to sixth grade, and I cleaned white women's floors for a living. I'm just a dum-dum," she'd moan to my grandfather whenever she felt he was ignoring her, which was often. Technically, he *was* ignoring her, but he ignored everyone who talked to him; he was deaf. He bought a hearing aid, but he turned it off minutes after he slipped it into his ear.

"I don't blame him," my mother said as my grandmother's voice screeched through the room.

While that act of deaf defiance provided my grandfather with inner peace, it also meant there were two levels of speaking in their house: an Indoor Voice (whisper) and a Talking to Pop-Pop Voice (yelling like someone was coming at you with a shotgun). My grandmother didn't approve of loud children, so during visits I spent most of the time sitting absolutely still, moving only to a chair when the plastic couch covering stuck to my body. Nana had no air-conditioner.

• • •

"We're not going to be living here long," my mother said as she un-packed our few things. Our new home was her old bedroom, a small museum of 1960s artifacts. I found a space in between her Afro-pick sculpture and STUDENTS FOR JFK button to lay my book bag down.

Five minutes into unpacking, Nana called up through the vent.

"What are you doing?" she yelled. "Come down here and watch television with me!"

All that worrying about oven-dried hair. I forgot to think about how much boring television I'd be forced to watch at Nana's. Well, not really watching television, more like talking to televi-sion. Whenever one of Nana's favorite shows was on, she'd yell at the screen, her commentary drowning out the program.

If the news was on and there was a report of a mugging but no police sketch of the robber, she'd yell, "You know he's white, be-cause if he was black they'd have showed it! That's just how white people do black people." She'd sigh, waves of bitterness and anger filling the small living room. I hated watching the news with her. I was certain she believed that, being part white, I was also a bad person.

Game shows were a bit more fun. If Nana was watching a game show, her rules dictated that we drop everything to cheer for brown contestants. One night, I got out of cleaning dinner plates because an Indian man was on *Jeopardy!*

"Go on, brother, phrase it like a question!" my grandmother yelled.

"Nana, he's Indian, not black," I whispered to her.

"He's not what?" she replied, angry that I had taken her atten-tion away from the *Jeopardy!* board. "He *is* a black man. See, they al-ways put black people in the last space." She pointed to the third *Jeopardy!* podium.

I conceded and cheered Mr. Bhatia, hoping he would go on a winning streak so I'd never have to clear dishes again.

The only programs that required absolute silence were her "stories," the soap operas. From the time on the clock, I knew that was what my grandmother was watching when she called up through the vent. I would have chewed off my right foot not to have to go down to the living room. Watching soap operas was torture: The people talked too slowly, no one laughed, and none of the *Young and the Restless* characters had their own cereal.

As my mother started down the stairs, I told her I had to go to the bathroom but promised I'd be right down. I sat on the toilet trying to figure out how long I could stretch out my freedom before I got in trouble. Nana answered me by calling up through the vent again. "What are you getting into up there?"

I pulled up my pants and headed downstairs.

At the top of the stairs, I looked down at the living room. Nana was humming "Swing Low, Sweet Chariot" while trying to push herself up from the sofa. With one forceful shove, she finally rose and stumbled to the china cabinet that housed her army of orange medicine bottles. She stood in front of her cabinet reading the pill names and adding commentary. "No, that one is for my arthur-eye-tis; I don't take that one until dinnertime."

She was blocking my path to the sofa. I knew I would be stuck on the steps until she moved, so I offered up my assistance.

"Do you need me to get something for you, Grandmom?"

Her eyes locked on mine. "Vertigo!" she screeched back at me. She rocked slightly before throwing her upper body into the banister pole. "Vertigo!" she screamed again, and gripped the pole like it was the only stable tree in a hurricane.

My mother jumped up to help her. That wasn't enough.

"Vertigo, John!" Nana screamed in her Talking to Pop-Pop Voice. My grandfather slowly rose from his seat, and the three of us gently guided her back to her permanently indented cushion on the sofa.

Until I was eleven, because of my grandmother, I thought *Vertigo!* was what you shouted whenever you were struck with sudden pain. When I experienced my first menstrual cramps, my mother yelled to me to hurry up and get ready for school. I called back, "Vertigo!" and got in trouble because she thought I was mocking her mother.

After my grandmother's vertigo subsided, she picked up her "lottery book," a small reporter's notepad in which she had recorded every Pennsylvania daily lottery number since 1949. She was certain there was a pattern to the lottery numbers, and if she could just crack the code she'd be a millionaire. While she was flipping through her pages, a preview for the news came on. I got nervous—I wasn't ready to be hated. I asked my mother if I could go outside.

"Yes."

Yes? That's when I knew things had changed and Nana's house was truly our new home. Usually, the farthest outside I was allowed to go was sitting on the enclosed front porch with Nana as she surveyed the block, talking about how downhill it had all gone.

Before my mother could change her mind, I bolted toward the door like I was making a prison break. I ran down the street toward three girls jumping rope, only with two ropes instead of one.

Two ropes should be just as easy, I tried to convince myself, watching the ropes swing like manic egg beaters.

"Big Mac, Filet of Fish," the girls chanted in unison. They all had braids like mine, except theirs lay flat on their scalps, as if they were glued down. Each tiny braid ended with beads and aluminum foil. When a girl jumped into the ropes, the sun danced off the aluminum and made her head seem to be surrounded by a universe of tiny stars.

I immediately wanted to be a Star Girl, to look like a planetarium when I jumped. I got up the nerve to ask if I could play.

"You got ends," one girl said, handing me the ends of the wiry clothesline. I would have preferred to start off jumping, bobbing my head as I bounced, practicing for my day as a Star Girl, but since I was the new arrival, I had to start at the bottom. I started spinning my end of the ropes like I'd observed them doing. The girl who had handed them off to me finessed her way into the rope and started jumping. The fast-food chant began—"Big Mac, Filet"—and stopped abruptly when she missed her footing.

"Dag, Kim, you only got to Filet!" my co-turner called out.

Kim stomped out of the rope. "That's 'cause she's double-handed!" Kim replied. I knew the *she* was me. Everyone looked at me. Confused, I looked at my hands.

Double-handed? Did they mean double-jointed? I knew all about that; my next-door neighbor could bend her pinky back until it touched her thumb. If they didn't mean double-jointed, what did they mean? Should I show them that I wasn't double-jointed? Should I tell them they were making the game more confusing than it needs to be by using two ropes and a McDonald's commercial as a counting system?

From the looks on their faces, I was the oddball, so I refrained from offering my jump-rope suggestions. I'd wait until they accepted me to try to change them.

"Here, try again," Kim said. I started turning the ropes. Keisha, a tall bronze girl shaped like a pogo stick with tiny breasts, entered. She held one arm protectively over her breast buds as she jumped. I studied her feet as I turned. She made it all the way to "Apple Pie."

"Have you ever jumped double Dutch before?" Keisha asked, snatching the ends from my hands.

Everyone was annoyed with me, but it was finally my chance to jump. *This is my chance to prove myself. God, please let me make it past Filet.*

The ropes slapped the ground, awaiting my entrance. I held my breath and leapt in with all the grace of a drunk jumping off a cliff. My arms flailed at my sides. My legs landed heavy on the rope as if I had cement in my shoes.

"Big," all three girls called out unenthusiastically.

I didn't even make it to "Mac." I couldn't even get a whole burger.

"Let her get a freebie," Kim said, enlightening me on two double-Dutch rules. One: She was in charge because it was her rope. Two: If a jumper can't get past the first word of the McDonald's jingle, it must be everyone involved's fault (no one is that untalented); thus the jumper gets a second try.

The ropes spun again. This time I tried to imitate how the other girls looked when they jumped in. I scowled at the ropes like they had killed my firstborn. I put my arm protectively across breasts I didn't have yet. I swayed my body back and forth to the timing of the rope turns, timing out my entrance in my head. *Jump now! No, wait. Jump now! No, wait! Just do it!*

I jumped in, and a sharp pain flew across my forehead. I fell backward to the cement, heard a popping sound, and saw a barrette launch into the street and hit the tire of the G bus, which had stopped to discharge passengers.

I tried to get up, but when I moved it felt like someone was pulling a zipper through my hair. When I could think past the pain, I deduced that one of the ropes had smacked me in the forehead, traveled along my head, and got tangled in my braid. My curly hair tends to spiral around anything close to it, and with the barrette no longer holding the ends of the braid together, the individual strands were coiling around the rope.

Butt cheeks still on the cement, I tried to yank my head out of the rope. The girls, stunned stiff with looks of pity until this point, dropped the ends and rushed to unravel me from the clothesline.

"No, Kim, you untwist and I'll hold her head straight!" Nikki yelled, cradling my head in her hands. "Twist the rope to the left, *then* to the right! Go *with* the braid!" she yelled.

I looked up at her helplessly as she commandeered the double-Dutch surgery. I was one notch above a shivering dog floating down an icy stream yelping at the amateur rescue squad. Perhaps I could have been the feel-good story on the evening news: *Oreo kid moves to hood, gets curly Oreo hair caught in rope, and is freed by local girls.* They'd interview Kim.

"No, I don't consider myself a hero," she'd say, explaining that anyone in her situation would have done the same thing.

While looking up at them unraveling me, I wondered how the Star-haired girls hadn't met this same fate. It must be the flat braids, I reasoned. If your braids fling around loose, you were bound to get ensnared by clothesline.

"You got it!" Nikki yelled. "She's free!"

"Ick, there's a bunch of hair on my rope!" Kim said.

Nikki released my head. "Where are you from?" she asked, her tone indicating that she was asking a grander question, like "Where is your type of person manufactured?" as opposed to which house I lived in. Even though I knew this, I turned my sore head slightly and pointed to my grandmother's house, where I saw my mother coming onto the porch. I used her as an excuse to bow out gracefully.

"Well, it was nice meeting you-all. I'm going to go home now," I said, then remembered my manners, "And thank you all for untangling me."

They said nothing.

I walked toward my mother and left the Star Girls confused, holding a very hairy jump rope.

"You made some new friends?" my mother asked as I approached, taking my Walkman headphones off her ears.

"I don't think so," I replied.

"What happened to your hair?" my mother asked suspiciously. She turned my head to the side and fingered my fresh forehead welt. "What happened to your face? Where's your barrette? Which one stole it? Oh, God, I have to get you out of this neighbor—"

"Nobody hit me," I said, trying to calm her down. "My hair got caught in the rope. I need tinfoil-star hair like those girls to jump double Dutch."

My mother wrinkled her brow and asked me to repeat myself. I pointed to the girls I'd just been playing with. She cocked her head, trying to analyze if I was lying. She accepted my answer, then looked over at the girls.

My mother exploded into laughter. "Those are called cornrows, darling," she explained.

"Can you do my hair like that tomorrow?"

"I don't know how."

"But didn't you grow up on this block?"

"No one in our family knows how to cornrow, honey," my mother said, and this time, I wrinkled my brow at her. How could she have grown up on this block and not know how to cornrow? Shouldn't everyone on this block know how to do that? Did she not know how to jump double Dutch either? Is that why she had to marry a white man?

My mother handed me the Walkman. I came up with a new strategy: If I couldn't get cornrows, I would use my radio technology to gain access to friends. The Walkman had just hit the marketplace, and no one else I knew had one. Who wouldn't want to be friends with a girl with a Walkman?

I excused myself from the steps and ran back over to the three girls, Walkman on, bobbing my head slowly to "Up Where We Belong."

My plan started working. "Can I listen?" Kim asked, dropping her spinning clothesline, more interested in what was on my head. I put the headphones over her ears.

Kim listened for a few seconds and then snatched the headphones off and held them away from her body like they were transmitting a satanic broadcast. "Who is this?" she asked, my earphones dangling from her fingertips.

"Joe Cocker," I replied. I remembered the singer's name because the boys in my class would always say his last name, point to their crotches, and break out into laughter.

"Keisha, listen to this," she said, putting my headphones on Keisha's ears. Keisha recoiled as Kim did. She howled, clutched her stomach, and gasped for air. Kim then repeated the scene with Nikki, who topped Keisha's laugh by jolting her body like thousands of tiny invisible hands were tickling her.

"Why are you listening to this white station? You should be listening to Power Ninety-nine," Kim said, putting the headphones back on and adjusting the radio dial a few notches. She listened to some music for a few seconds and then handed the Walkman back to me.

"This music is better," she said, putting the headphones back on my ears.

All three girls looked at me to see if I approved. I did.

"I like this," I said, not really having enough time to decide if that was true. As the Star Girls looked on, I smiled and tapped my foot, hoping I could catch the beat.

Doo-Doo Head

African-American women each spend two to three times more on hair care and beauty than women of other races, totaling $1.16 billion annually.

—*Data from the Hunter-Miller Group,
a market research firm*

Living in an all-black neighborhood, I soon learned the importance of hair and found that most black people categorized mine as *good*. My mother had many descriptive names for my hair, but *good* was not even close to being one of them.

From the time my hair started sprouting, my mother would style my hair the same way every day. She'd sit me between her legs, part my hair down the middle (which took about half an hour in itself), and put each half of my hair into a ponytail holder. She'd then braid both ponytails and hold the end of the finished braid with her thumb and forefinger while opening a plastic barrette with her teeth. Finally, she'd snap the barrette on the end and flatten any flyaway strands with Luster's Pink Lotion.

Those braids would last from two to three hours. On other kids, braids were the cactus version of hairstyles: very little maintenance and they still looked good. My hair expands like a balloon if there is any humidity. If the kid sitting next to me spills his juice box—poof—the liquid on the floor causes my hair to enlarge. Every single day I'd leave the house with two braids and two barrettes and sometime between the Pledge of Allegiance and the first bathroom break one of my barrettes would pop off, unable to sustain my swelling, expanding hair.

The first time my barrette flew off, Sister Mary let me look for it. The second time, she tolerated the boys' laughter as they ducked to avoid my airborne barrette. The third time—when my plastic barrette flipped behind the radiator and melted, making the room smell so bad we had to evacuate and have class in the church—she sent a letter home with me, suggesting a safer hairstyle.

After the note, my frugal mother tried to cut my hair according to a do-it-yourself book she borrowed from the library. Pink faces, not much lighter than mine, stared up from the pages. She sectioned off and started chopping into my hair with craft scissors, brushing back beads of sweat and taking deep breaths.

"We have to find a Russian Jew!" she'd scream in frustration, throwing the scissors down. Apparently, one of her coworkers told her that Jewish people, especially ones from Russia, have a grade of hair like mine.

Finally, after hours of parting and cutting, being unable to find a salon in the yellow pages with a "We specialize in Russian-Jewish hair!" ad, she surveyed my head and sighed. "I guess this is all right."

It was not all right. I looked as if she'd bent me over the sink, thrown my hair into the garbage disposal, and powered it on. Without my Catholic school uniform, I looked homeless. I had an AfroCurlMushroom; it was shaped like a chef's hat, with random pieces very blunt cut and some long pieces in the back.

After sleeping on it, my mother decided to keep me home from school the next day and call in some hair troops. "They'll arrest me if I send you out looking like that," she said. She wasn't far off. (Many years later my brother's wife told me that her white mother would try to style her hair using a thin-tooth comb made for fine hair. Desiree would squeal like a pig as the comb snagged its way down her tight curls. The neighbors, hearing Desiree's screams, assumed that her white mother was abusing her and called the authorities. Several combs later, Social Services showed up on the doorstep. They wrote it up as just another case of white mother, black child, and let Desiree remain in her custody.)

Luckily, no one called the cops when my mother Grace Jones'd my hair, but no one, even salons in the best part of the city, could offer a solution to fix it either. Even after it grew back in, when she took me around from hairdresser to hairdresser, no one wanted to touch my hair. Instead, they offered suggestions.

"Take her to the Puerto Rican neighborhood, they have crazy hair like hers," the local hairdresser said.

"I *think* I can work with her texture, but I'd have to charge you five times my rate because it's going to take all day," a high-class stylist said.

The last place my mother tried was the Hair Cuttery, figuring it would be discrimination if they refused to do my hair. Apparently, it's not, so long as they are polite about it. After the all-white staff corrected their initial looks of shock, the only available stylist looked closely at my scalp and declared that I had the most hair follicles she had ever seen. "I'm so sorry. Try a shop that does relaxers," she said, handing me a Blow Pop and walking us to the door.

After the double-Dutch incident on 56th Street, my mother decided to give in and pay someone to cornrow my hair. Actually, a young neighborhood woman, Crystal, embarrassed her into doing it. "Your daughter looks a mess. If I braid it, you won't have to deal with it for a month. Just rub a Q-Tip on the scalp with some shampoo, and you're good to go," Crystal said, offering her best sales pitch. My mother made an appointment and Crystal was set to braid my hair in our bedroom the next day.

Once upstairs, when Crystal took her tools and hair grease out, my mother tried to haggle over the price. Crystal noticed the VCR my mother had taken from our old house. My mother asked Crystal if she wanted the VCR instead of the money. They bartered for a while and finally the destiny of my hair was handed over along with a VCR and two Amos and Andy tapes. I thought that was outrageous, but to my mother, the VCR was worth nothing and control over my hair was priceless.

"Oh, girl, you have a lot of hair!" Crystal said as I sat on the floor between her legs. She started putting razor-thin parts in my hair with a comb and then twisted my scalp into tiny knots. After four hours, Crystal said her arms were hurting and called in her sister to help finish. My grandmother, who never visited the third floor, preferring to yell through the vents when she needed to reach us, came up to watch the progress and the two young girls in her house. She flipped when she saw both of them with their hands in my hair.

"No, don't let two people braid your hair at once. Y'all know that's not right. Too many cooks in the pot!" she screamed, looking at me like I had "666" on my scalp. Crystal's sister, now chastised, sat on the bed and let Crystal finish. I wondered if I was now under a spell or if my hair would suddenly turn "bad."

If I was cursed by the two cooks in my hair, it was worth it, because Crystal left me with a head full of tiny braids lying flat across my head. Each braid was capped off with wooden beads held in place by small pieces of aluminum foil. Being downgraded to living without AC became bearable. I could face the hot days that had crept up on us by sitting in front of my grandmother's fan with the cool air hitting the exposed areas of my scalp.

Unfortunately, my hair joy was short-lived because no one bothered to tell me the rules of life with braids. Certainly I had noticed that the black girls kept their heads bobbing above water in the city swimming pool, but they all seemed to do it, not just the black girls with braids. I had no idea that a different hairstyle meant that I should follow the "head above water" rule, so I did what I'd always done as soon as the lifeguard blew the whistle: I dove into the pool cannonball style, getting an automatic wedgie along with a head full of water.

Swimming back to the surface, I noticed that the water was extra sparkly around my head. The foil had rocketed off my hair when I hit the water and was now floating in the water near my face.

Underwater, a boy swam by me then blasted to the surface with a face full of snot. He pointed at me and screamed, "Ewww, she doodooed in the water!" I looked down and saw my wooden beads in an almost perfect pile under my feet.

"She doodooed! Look, y'all, she doodooed!" the boy called out, leading a swimming tour around my legs. The lifeguard stared at me in disgust and yelled to another lifeguard, "We got a pooper!"

I knew what was coming. If they cleared the pool out and people thought it was because I had an underwater bowel movement, I would never be able to show my face at the pool again. "It's just my beads!" I yelled out, holding up the one braid that still had a rack of beaks on it.

With this revelation, the boys started diving under me to retrieve my beads, not to give them back to me but to the cutest girls, who of course could not dive for their own beads because they couldn't get their hair wet. The pretty girls with the perfect hair bobbed above the water like beautiful lily pads as I tried to dive and reclaim some of the beads I'd waited so long for.

Only getting two beads back, I crawled out of the pool and walked home. My mother screamed when she saw my hair. She'd lost a VCR and two tapes, and my hair was worse than when we'd started. She had to cut out the remaining beads; the curls and the wetness had strangled them.

We sat up all night as she washed my hair and tried to pull it straight back into her original two-braid style. That style lasted a record four hours the next day, which my mother took as a sign from God that we should just leave my hair alone.

Patron Saint of White Fathers

Martin of Porres is the only known biracial patron saint. He is also known as Martin of Charity and the Saint of the Broom (for his devotion to his work, no matter how menial).

—*Catholic-Forum.com (www.catholic-forum.com/ saints/saintm02.htm)*

"Aren't you excited to go to your new school?" my mother said, dragging me out of bed by one arm.

I clutched the headboard. "Please don't make me go, I have a fever," I wailed.

"There's going to be a fever on your butt if you don't get in the shower," my mother replied. I still wouldn't budge. I preferred a spanking over going to a new school.

I had no idea what this new school would be like, but I wanted to go back to my old one, where I knew my place in the pecking order. Being biracial, two years younger than the other students in my grade, and non-Catholic, I knew I was stuck as a Middle: not cool enough for the popular kids but not dorky enough that they constantly picked on me to maintain their popularity. It was comfortable, almost like being invisible.

"Young lady, you will go to school and get an education. That's the one thing a man can't take away from you when he declares bankruptcy and every single thing is in both names," my mother said, clenching her teeth.

Like separate bedrooms and cable television, my mother's flowery "you're beautiful and everyone will love you" speeches were a thing of our two-parent-home past. A conversation getting dressed for school now could easily devolve into a conversation about the benefit of separate checking accounts.

I got up. My mother had laid out the same school uniform I'd worn to St. Irenaeus. As I put on the familiar navy-blue tunic, I was grateful that at least one thing was staying the same.

If you want to guarantee a horrible time at a party, show up wearing the wrong dress. When my new teacher, Miss Shannon, escorted me into her fourth-grade classroom and had my new classmates introduce themselves, no one looked me in the face. Instead, they said their names to my solid-blue uniform. Everyone looked offended by me, as if I'd worn a Cinderella costume to their grandmother's funeral.

At recess, the girls gathered around me like moths to light. As they stood around me, each girl tried to shout out her questions a little louder than the next, like a schoolyard press conference. *Why are you wearing that uniform? Did the store sell you the wrong uniform? Are you going to wear that uniform tomorrow? Did you keep the receipt so you can return that wrong uniform?*

I answered the questions as fast as I could. I was happy for some attention, even if it was to how weirdly I was dressed. Suddenly, the circle parted and Maureen, a girl I recognized from the back of my new classroom, approached me.

If Martians had landed in that fourth-grade class and asked to be taken to the leader, everyone would have pointed to Maureen. She was as tall as Miss Shannon, and everyone treated her with the same reverence. Maureen looked like a woman squeezed into a child's uniform, someone my mother might work with or my father might have dated. While everyone else sported braids, Maureen's hair was straight, like a model in a Dark and Lovely ad. She stood over me and blocked out the sun. "Can you jump double Dutch?" Maureen asked, shifting her jaw.

"I'm not very good," I answered.

Without further ado, Maureen walked away, taking the press conference with her.

Most of my classmates watched Maureen's double-Dutch game from the sidelines. They hung on the wall of the school with their bodies posed nonchalantly, but their eyes begged for a chance to get a jump. A few girls gave up and headed to the chalk hopscotch board. I followed them. Janine, a girl with about the same complexion as mine, was about to throw the stone. I shuffled over and put my mouth close to her ear.

"Is your dad or your mom white?" I whispered. I was certain Janine was mixed because on the rare occasion I saw a woman with full lips, thick black hair, and a very light complexion in our old neighborhood, I'd ask my mother, "Is she mixed?" to which my mother would always reply yes. Spot the Mixed Woman was one of my favorite childhood games.

I thought I had the whole biracial thing figured out. People with my complexion—Lisa Thomas-Laury, David Hasselhoff, Janine, my younger brother—were mixed, and when I spotted enough of them I'd gather them up so we could hang out in our own group like black and white people did.

Janine's eyes narrowed into angry slits. "Is *who* white?" she asked.

I repeated the question in a lower tone to hint at the secrecy of my biracial unity plan. In response, Janine puffed her cheeks out like a blowfish, slammed the hopscotch rock down, and stomped away. Their hopscotch game halted, the other players stared at me.

"What's her problem?" I asked, flipping my hair back in feigned coolness.

"You're about to get your butt kicked," one girl offered. She pointed behind me. I turned and saw Janine talking to Maureen. Maureen's mouth dropped along with her rope. Instantly, she started walking toward me, a crew of girls bringing up the rear, like some Catholic production of *West Side Story*.

Maureen stood directly in front of me. Her face was so close to mine that if I'd stuck out my tongue I could have licked her nose.

I closed my eyes. *I am going to die. I'm going to die right here in the schoolyard.*

"Did you call my friend white?" Maureen asked. Behind her, the all-girl ass-kicking squad shifted nervously on their feet. One girl cracked her knuckles.

"No. I asked her if she was *half* white."

"Why would you ask her that?"

"Because my dad is white."

Maureen flicked her hand dismissively. "You're buggin'," she said, and turned to the girls, laughing. The group, seeing their leader laugh, knew what to do. They fell over one another, cackling and clutching their chests as if their lungs were about to burst. "She's buggin'!" several girls called out, echoing Maureen.

"Ladies! Ladies! This is a schoolyard, not a zoo!" Miss Shannon yelled from the other side of the yard. Chastised, the girls lowered their volume. I wanted them to laugh again. Laughing people can't throw punches.

"Your dad ain't white!" Maureen said.

"Yeah, your dad ain't white," another girl yelled.

"He better not be white!" someone called out. "I drank behind you at the water fountain, and I don't drink after white people!"

"If your dad was white, you'd be rich like Arnold and Willis and could afford the right uniform!" someone observed astutely.

"True, true, they always have nice clothes on *Diff'rent Strokes*," someone else yelled.

I knew, no matter how much I wanted to cry, I couldn't let them see that they had hurt me. I didn't know I could probably have ended it right there by falling in line behind Maureen and agreeing with the reality she had chosen to give me. If Maureen wanted to rearrange my family tree, I was supposed to stand there and catch the branches as she sawed them off.

I thought Maureen was just pretending not to believe me so she'd have an excuse to whip my behind. I didn't know that ten-year-olds who lived in West Philly didn't come in contact with too many white men. There were no white male teachers at the school. No white male students. White men were read about, prayed to, and watched on television. They weren't people you hung out with. They certainly weren't your fathers.

"If your dad is white, bring him in to school!" Maureen yelled.

"Yeah, bring him to school!" the backup fighters sang out.

I pictured how smoothly school life would go if that were possible. On the next show-and-tell day, Miss Shannon would say, "Thanks, Jahiem, for bringing in your Hot Wheels Mechanic Garage. Next, Angela will present her Caucasian Father." *Ooh, can I play with him?* the whole class would shout.

"I can't bring him in because I don't live with him anymore!" I screamed.

Maureen's eyes rolled back in her head and she stuck an open palm in my face. *Yes, sure. How convenient that you had a white dad and you can't bring him in because you don't live with him anymore.*

Dana, a thin girl with a thick country accent, waved her arms in the air. She had an urgent announcement that might settle this inquisition. "Wait, wait, wait, y'all!" She stepped between Maureen and myself. "Is your dad white-*white* like Miss Shannon or white like light-skinned?"

"He's like Miss Shannon, except a little whiter," I said.

That was it. I had blown my last chance to color my dad. Dana threw her skinny arms in the air in a sign of surrender and walked back over to the double-Dutch ropes.

"You're a liar," Janine announced, and looked up at Maureen like she was expecting a pat on the head and a biscuit for bringing a person of such low morality to her leader's attention.

Maureen punched her fist into her palm. "If you don't bring your dad to school, you have to give me a fair one!"

"Yeah, a fair one!" the girls chimed in.

"How was your first day of school, honey?" my mother asked. We were watching *Wheel of Fortune* with my grandmother. A black woman had just landed on Bankrupt.

My grandmother moaned. "Awww, shoot. This game is racist. How come Bankrupt is the only black space on the wheel?"

"Mom, I don't really like that school. The teacher said I can't come back if I don't have the right uniform," I lied, figuring if I couldn't produce a white dad, I had a better chance of surviving if I dressed according to regulation.

"Angela, I am not buying a uniform just for one month of school," my mother replied. "Please promise me that when you have a job you won't spend money on anything except things that are absolutely necessary, because if your husband doesn't pay child support you'll be stuck."

"White people love Vanna White. She got a body like a colored woman," my grandmother mumbled.

"Please, Mom. I don't want people to tease me," I begged.

"Did someone say something about your uniform? Because if they did, they can buy you a new uniform or they can take their little butts over to your dad's house and tell *him* you need a new uniform."

My grandmother shifted in her seat. "Can y'all quiet down? The colored gal is about to solve the puzzle."

I excused myself and I went upstairs to search for a photo of my father. *I'll show that to Maureen and everything will be cool,* I thought.

Of course, I didn't stop to think that when women leave their husbands, the last thing on the "to pack" list are photos of him. I tore the third-floor bedroom up: I rummaged through dressers, I crawled under the bed, I dumped out shoeboxes full of receipts.

An hour later, I was bathed in sweat and exhausted. Frustrated and desperate, I picked up my mother's purse, hoping to find a wallet-size of their days as a happy couple. My mother must have had a handbag motion detector installed, because as soon as the last penny fell from the bottom of her purse, she appeared in the doorway.

"Are you stealing from me?" my mom said, grabbing her purse and sweeping the contents back into it. "Did you know that in China they cut your fingers off for stealing?"

I started crying. Maureen was going to kill me, and this would be the last day I'd ever see my mother. "I was just looking for a photo of Daddy," I said, tears dripping on the collar of my uniform.

My mom's eyes filled with water. "Awww, honey," she said, mistakenly assuming that I was exhibiting signs of Broken Home Syndrome.

The next morning, the Yellow Pages was on the bed, opened up to CHILD PSYCHIATRISTS.

"I'm picking you up early today. You're going to talk to a counselor," she said, giving me another look of pity to add to all the ones I'd received the previous day when Maureen announced that she was giving me a "fair one." I was unsure of what a counselor was, but I didn't care if my mother had said I was going to a dentist who didn't use anesthetic. I was leaving school early, which meant less time to spend hiding in the school basement (my plan B to escape a fight).

Still, I had to get through a half day. When I got to the schoolyard, I saw Maureen fake-boxing with two sixth-graders. Her face perked up when she spotted me trying to tiptoe toward the safety of Miss Shannon. Maureen pointed to me, and the two sixth-graders jogged toward me and blocked my path.

"I'm Keyana. Janine, the girl you called white, is my play cousin," the taller girl said. I thought it odd but weirdly polite that she would introduce herself before fighting.

"You can't come to a new school and bust on somebody, then lie about your dad and not get a fair one," Keyana's friend added. She paused and looked at me expectantly, as if I had one last chance to say something to change her mind.

All I could do was ball my fists up and concentrate on holding back my tears. Keyana started slicking her hair into a ponytail. Her friend unfastened her gold hoop earrings and pinned them to her uniform collar.

I looked up to the church roof. I tried to will the Virgin Mary statue into toppling off the building and knocking the girls over like bowling pins. Of course, the Virgin was not going to be my accomplice in a homicide; she'd rather stand there with pigeons on her head.

"Why you look so scared? You don't have to fight both of us. Just me," Keyana said.

As Keyana stepped closer to me, I again looked up at Mary and my mind flashed back to my old school and the boys' fights. I remembered the one boy who was often teased but never hit: Sean, the mentally disabled/retarded/slow boy.

"Why you not saying anything?" the sidekick asked, laughing.

"Bunk youuu," I replied, slurring my words and elongating my vowels in my best imitation of Sean.

"What did you say?" Keyana asked.

"Bunk youuuuu!" I screamed, slumping one side of my body and keeping my mouth open for a few seconds after the words had come out.

Keyana locked eyes with me and squinted as if she was trying to bring my face back in focus. I put up two limp fists, like a handicapped Rocky.

"Bunk yoouuuu!" I screamed again.

"She's retarded!" the sidekick exclaimed, backing away from me as if retardation were contagious. Keyana walked backward for a few steps, then they both spun around and ran toward Maureen, throwing their hands up in her face.

"You didn't tell us she was retarded! That's messed up!" they yelled. Just as Maureen looked over toward me, the head nun rang the bell, indicating it was time to line up and go inside. I gripped my rosary beads before heading inside. Maureen stared at me for three straight hours until my mother arrived to pick me up.

The counseling center was a row house in the middle of a regular West Philadelphia block, the only home with white people sitting on the porch. The waiting room was decorated with posters I didn't understand.

One poster looked like the universal NO SMOKING sign, except instead of a cigarette with a slash through it there was a wire hanger.

No hangers? What does that mean? Maybe our counselor hates hanging up clothes.

Another poster featured two men in a passionate embrace.

"Mom, why are those guys French-kissing?" I asked.

"Because . . . because they are good friends," my mother replied.

Our counselor called us into her office. She was a middle-aged hippie, the perfect spokeswoman for Birkenstocks and loose-fitting skirts. She insisted I call her Sue (instead of Miss Sue like my mother said), and once I was seated on her couch she handed me markers and asked me to draw a picture of my family.

I drew my mother, brother, and myself and then, off to the side, another version of myself being punched in the face by girls in plaid uniforms.

"Who are the girls in plaid?" Sue asked.

I spilled everything, from my hopscotch racial faux pas to my clash with Janine's play cousin.

". . . so I had to act like a 'tard!" I finished. I looked over at my mother and immediately corrected myself. "I mean retarded," I said, dropping my head to the floor.

"I had no idea," my mother said cautiously to Sue, as if making sure there was no additional charge for bringing in a truckload of extra problems.

"Wow, what a smart girl you were to act retarded!" Sue exclaimed, and turned to my mother. "We're going to need quite a few more sessions."

While driving back to my grandmother's house, my mother asked what would make the rest of the school year go easier for me.

"Please come tell Maureen that my dad is white," I said.

"Lord, give me strength," my mother murmured.

• • •

The next day, my mother marched into the schoolyard with me. "That's Maureen!" I said. My mom yanked me toward her and stood eye to eye with my bully.

"Angela says that you don't believe her dad is white." Maureen opened her mouth to reply, but my mother cut her off. "Her father is just as white as I am black. If you have any other questions you want to ask about her family, you ask me. Got it?" With my mother yelling at her, Maureen shrank before my eyes. She was just an eleven-year-old in a training bra that I had outbullied with the ultimate weapon: an angry, overworked, single black mother.

Maureen kept her eyes to the ground, looking like she wanted to find a crack in the cement so she could crawl into it and hide. My mother left her and walked over to talk to Miss Shannon. Maureen, in a last-ditch attempt to save face in front of her followers, glanced at my mother and sucked her teeth.

As I was about to join my mother, Maureen grabbed me by the arm. I blocked my face, prepared for the punch.

"You got ends," she said, holding out her end of the rope. Suspiciously, I grabbed the double-Dutch olive branch and started turning. Not five minutes into the game, another classmate, Erica, who had recently taken my spot in the front row by claiming she couldn't see the board, accused me of being double-handed.

"Erica, get some glasses 'cause you blind!" Maureen screamed. It's like I really *was* retarded/mentally disabled/slow Sean, suddenly tight with the class bully. I promised myself I would abuse my Maureen-protected status for as long as I had it.

"Call me double-handed again and you'll have to give me a fair one," I whispered to Erica.

Once in the classroom, Miss Shannon startled us all with a bold announcement. "We're going to start religion class a little late. I want to talk about race and differences," she said.

Huh? It's not February, why are we talking about race stuff? Oh, God, my mother must have told her what Maureen did. Please don't single me out, Miss Shannon. I finally got Maureen to be my friend. Let it drop, lady!

"What color am I?" Miss Shannon asked the class.

"White!" the class clown, Rufus, called out without raising his hand. He was very excited to be able to answer a question correctly.

"Yes. I'm white," Miss Shannon said. "And what color is Charmaine?" she asked. Charmaine was a light-skinned girl with hazel eyes and more beads in her hair than hair. Every time she moved her head, it sounded like the beginning of a mariachi tune.

"White!" Rufus called out again, laughing. This time he knew he was wrong, but emboldened by one correct answer, he couldn't resist going for a quick second dose of attention.

Charmaine whipped her head around and glared at Rufus. "You white! Your mother white!"

"Charmaine, be quiet!" Miss Shannon said.

"I ain't white!" Charmaine said. She folded her arms across her chest and slid down in her seat.

Miss Shannon was in over her head. She didn't know that being called white was a dis. Actually, I'm not sure she knew how to give a lesson on race. For ten minutes, she just called the names of various civil rights activists and musicians and then asked what race the person was. When she finished running down the entire Motown roster ("and what color is Jermaine Jackson?") she summed up her lesson: "Black and white people can do anything, and they can do it together."

Maureen's hand shot into the air. "Black people can't do anything! My mother said they can't be president."

Miss Shannon clapped her hands against her cheeks. "Why, Maureen, that's horrible! Of course a black person could be president," she said. "Maybe what your mom meant is that we haven't had a black president yet!"

"No," Maureen replied. "My mom said *never*. She said if it does happen, he'll be shot the next day. Bam!" Maureen said, pointing a fake gun at Miss Shannon.

Miss Shannon's mouth opened, but nothing came out.

Janine raised her hand and broke Miss Shannon's silence. "I know something else black people can't be! They can't be nuns!"

Miss Shannon's face lit up. "There are indeed black nuns!" she said, smiling. With murmurs of disbelief moving through the classroom, Miss Shannon took out Field Trip forms from her desk and passed them out. "We'll just have to go see one, won't we?"

As Miss Shannon passed a packet down each row, she caught my eye. *If she asks me to get up and say a few words, I'm running out of this room and going home,* I thought.

"Angela," she said, "make sure everyone in the class gives you a big thank-you. You're the reason we get to go on this field trip."

With those words, Ms. Shannon transformed me into the most popular girl in class. I was the magic new girl with the white dad and the ability to get them out of school to see black nuns.

The day of the field trip, Maureen saved a space for me on the school bus. When we hopped off the bus at the entrance to the convent grounds, Maureen shouted, " 'Scuse me, where's the black sister?" to the first nun we saw.

"Maureen!" Miss Shannon exclaimed, embarrassed.

The nun laughed and led our group to the convent entrance. She told us to wait as she went inside. A few moments later, a black nun popped her head out of an upstairs window like a cuckoo clock bird. She looked a bit irritated, as if someone was always interrupting her prayers to get her to wave at groups of disbelieving schoolchildren.

"She's too pretty to be a nun. She could get a man," Maureen announced to the group. I agreed, even though I'd never thought of nuns joining the convent because they were ugly.

No one paid attention for the rest of the trip. We were all giggling in excitement at seeing a real live black nun.

"Still, that don't mean a black person can be president," Maureen said, as we boarded the bus to ride home. "A nun I can understand, because nobody shoots nuns." Before she boarded the bus, she pointed an imaginary gun at the convent window.

• • •

"We have a surprise for you!" Sue said, clasping her hands together.

It was our fifth visit, and I was starting to tire of the counseling center. I didn't see the point. My problem was solved, Maureen was my friend. Plus, I felt like I was always letting Sue down. She'd give my mother and me homework assignments, but we could never get around to completing them. Two visits ago, she'd told my mother to take me to the park to show me how to turn double Dutch. That was a train wreck. It was impossible for my mother to turn the ropes with me and keep an eye on my brother. He tried to chase some geese and almost fell into the Schuylkill River. When my mother ran to save him, she slipped on goose droppings and twisted her ankle. "That's enough jump rope," she said, while I helped her limp to the car. She was in so much pain, I had to help hold the steering wheel steady while she drove home.

I also hated the way Sue always tried to pull "feelings" out of me. Every session she'd ask, "How does it feel to be mixed? Do you feel like you have to choose sides? Is it confusing?"

Who cares about feelings when you're popular? I thought. I wasn't confused at all, I just wanted people not to tease me. The more I insisted that I wasn't confused, the more Sue pressed me on it. "But I see the squiggly marks you drew around your head," she said, holding up my latest drawing.

Even when I told her the squiggly marks weren't symbolism, they were my version of cornrows, she prodded for feelings.

"Are you ready for the surprise?" Sue asked.

I nodded.

"The surprise is you're moving back to your old neighborhood so you can go back to your old school!" Sue exclaimed. "How do you feel about that?"

"Great," I lied.

I didn't tell Maureen I was leaving until the last day of school. My mother came to pick me up, the backseat of her car filled with boxes. Maureen hugged me like I was her daughter.

"Will we hang out over the summer?" Maureen asked.

"No, I won't see you this summer. I have to go back to my white school. It's better than this school," I said, just for the sake of being mean and making her feel as bad as she'd once made me feel. Of course now, in my paranoid old age, I'm afraid that telling her my white school was better than her school may have scarred her for life, made her hate white people, half-white people, or, more likely, herself. Whenever a black person is rude to me for no reason, I suck it up, figuring it's my Maureen karma.

"I'd tell you where it is, but I can't give directions to black people," I said, pronouncing the word *black* as if it were a disease.

I turned around to walk to the car. My mother was standing right over me, looking like she was trying to decide whether it would be easier to choke me with my uniform collar or bite my head off.

"If black people can't go to our old neighborhood, you'd better find somebody else to drive you." My mother planted herself down on the nuns' favorite bench and crossed her legs. "How are you, Maureen?" she asked, smiling at her.

"Mom, I—"

"I don't want to hear it," my mother said. "I don't know who told you that you were better than anyone else because you have a white dad, but let me tell you, you're just as black as me," she said. "One drop of black blood makes you black, young lady." And she left me with Maureen. Maureen looked shaken. It was the only time I'd ever seen her speechless.

"I'm sorry, Maureen," I said, and tried to give her a weak apology hug. She shoved me away.

When I got in the car, my mother turned up the radio, her sign that she didn't want to hear anything I had to say. To add to the punishment, she drove up and down almost every West Philadelphia street that day, as if what I'd said to Maureen was correct and her blackness kept her from knowing the directions back to Southwest Philly. I'd call out frustratedly, "Mom, you're supposed to turn here," and she'd slap her forehead.

"I'm so glad I have you in the car, I'd be so lost!" my mother said twenty times in ten minutes.

A half tank of gas later, the sight of a cop riding her bumper startled her into ceasing the role of Lost Black Driver. Since my father still held title to the car, we were driving on expired tags. We avoided interactions with cops like we were a drug mule family.

"Angie, crawl in the backseat and wave to the cop," my mother said.

I hesitated.

"Wave to the cop. If he pulls up and sees that you look part white, he'll understand why the car is registered to a Nissel. I can't afford a ticket," she said.

"But I'm not part white. You just said I'm all black."

"Please, Angela, just wave!" I obeyed and crawled into the backseat, waving and smiling like I was on a parade float. The cop drove off.

I stayed in the backseat, wondering if being half white was some kind of hidden superpower, one you only pulled out in times of danger. When was I supposed to hide it? With black schoolgirls? What happened if the wrong person found out? How come one drop of white blood doesn't make you white? Who made these rules, anyway, and why couldn't I get a copy of them?

"Mom, I want to see Sue," I announced. I was certain Sue would be proud of me. I finally had the confused feelings she'd been searching for.

My God Complex

"Tonight, the Academy is honoring both my people with *Fiddler on the Roof* and *Shaft*."

—*Sammy Davis, Jr.,*
black entertainer who converted to Judaism

"Why do you still go to that white church?" Miss Marlo, a frequent visitor to the beauty shop, asked my mother.

"Because the service is short. The priest has you in and out of there in forty-five minutes flat. Sometimes it's only a half-hour service if there's a game on that afternoon," my mother replied. "Plus, I don't have to buy dress clothes. You can wear jeans to that church!"

Every corner of Miss Lillian's basement salon responded with shouts of disbelief.

"She ain't lying," Miss Lillian chimed in. "Them people going to church look like they about to go camping."

"Well, that's just rude," Miss Marlo said, shaking her head. She was a diehard Southern Baptist and seemed more married to Jesus than any of my nuns. "If you can't dress up for the Lord, who can you dress up for?"

"God doesn't care what you wear," my mother said. "Plus, a lot of times, people in black churches aren't dressing for God. They're dressing for each other."

"Didn't you grow up in a black Baptist church?" Miss Marlo asked, the tone of her voice whispering *Heathen, sinner, sellout.*

"Your kids need to come to my church. They need a place with community."

My ears perked up. Did she say that Baptists had *community*? Why, I should go to Miss Marlo's church, declare my allegiance to Baptists, and get welcomed into this community. Why concentrate on racial acceptance when I can have a club where everyone has my back regardless of color as long as I worship their God? Besides, racial wars are so passé, so sixties. Holy wars are all the rage.

"Mom, I'd like to go to Miss Marlo's church," I chimed in.

"See, she don't even like your church," Miss Marlo said, folding her arms across her chest.

"Fine, she can go to your church," my mother said to Miss Marlo. "As long as I don't have to buy her a new dress. Shoot, I'm robbing Peter to pay Paul as it is."

Attending Eagle Rock Baptist Church required more clothing, hair, and makeup preparation than going to a transvestite prom.

Saturday night, Miss Marlo thumbed through my closet until she found the only church-suitable dress, a frilly yellow Easter getup from 1985 B.C. (Before Cleavage). When I modeled it, my eleven-year-old breasts almost burst out of the thin cotton. Miss Marlo quickly threw her shawl over them like she was trying to smother a fire.

After the shawl/Easter dress outfit was deemed acceptable, I ironed it and changed into my nightclothes, and Miss Marlo began braiding my hair. It took two hours, as Miss Marlo took several pauses to pluck her eyebrows and tend to the collard greens she was cooking to take to church. When she finished my hair, she asked where my mother kept her hair wraps. I didn't know what a hair wrap was.

"It's like a bonnet to keep your hair from getting messed up." Miss Marlo sighed. I could tell by her tone that she would have been annoyed if she had to get up and look for it, so I brought her back the closest thing I could find: my swimming cap.

She shook her head from side to side and laughed a little. "I guess that'll do. Your head might get kinda hot, though." Miss Marlo placed the swim cap over my braids and secured it with the chin strap.

I woke up early Sunday morning and showered (with my swim cap on, of course). Miss Marlo inspected my washing work. She licked her finger and then rubbed the corners of my eyes. It was bad enough when my mother cleaned my face like that, but it seemed doubly disgusting when done by a nonrelated hand.

"You're about the ashiest little high-yellow child I've ever seen," Miss Marlo declared. "Go grease your face and legs."

"*Grease* my face?" I asked, confused.

"Good Lord." She sighed and took a jar of Vaseline from her purse, scooped a dollop of the jelly out, and smeared it over every exposed part of my body. When I glanced into the mirror, I looked like I was made of wax. She handed me the pot of greens to carry, and it almost slid out of my hands.

From the outside, the church looked unassuming, a tiny red building in the middle of a beat-up block of stores. Once inside, I was greeted by a hurricane of sequined hats and matching change purses. The smell of our collard greens mixed with the burnt smell of freshly hot-combed hair. Women greeted each other with shouts and hugs, as if they hadn't seen each other in years.

Is this really a church? I wondered. Where are the stained-glass windows, and how come there are only six rows of pews? Is that podium and microphone supposed to be an altar? How . . . quaint. I questioned my decision to come; I wondered why God would visit such a shabby place when he had huge Catholic churches with air-conditioning to hang out in.

Plus, if I was looking for a group to have my back, these people were hardly the type. My brother and I were the only people in the church not eligible for AARP.

"Where's the priest?" I asked.

Miss Marlo pointed to a man of about sixty, one of only two men in the room. He was chatting with three women, dressed all in white. "He's not called a priest, he's a minister," Miss Marlo explained. There wasn't enough time to ask her all my other questions, like, Why were people greeting her as Sister Marlo when she wasn't a nun? Where were the altar boys? Who are these Sick and Shut-In members and why are they shut in? Did they lose their house keys?

"Jeez-us! Praise his name!" a woman in the front pew called out and walked up to the podium. A parade of women followed her, each walking up to the front of the church to unburden themselves of all the week's troubles—lost jobs, recent cancer diagnoses, cut-off electricity. When they sat back down, they looked quite a bit lighter, like they had thrown pounds of pain from their shoulders. Testifying, they called it. It seemed different from the testifying my mother was called on to do in family court.

A song began. Miss Marlo's brown hands shot up toward the white stucco ceiling; she opened and closed them as if she were grabbing for something just beyond her reach.

"Hal-le-lu-jah," she intoned.

"Praise him!" the woman next to me hollered. The loudness of her voice startled me. I stared at her, trying to prepare myself for the next outburst. The woman closed her eyes and then shot out of her seat. As she stood, her body jerked back and forth as if she were being hit by multiple cattle prods.

In response, I let out an extended scream and pulled my breast-covering shawl over my eyes. Our pew was rocking. The more the backs of her knees hit our bench, the louder I screamed.

Miss Marlo gripped my hand. "Calm down, it's okay, she just got the Holy Ghost," she said. That gave me enough courage to pull my shawl down so it only covered my nose and mouth. The entire church was staring at me like, *Who's the screamer in the burka?*

My brother, in a daring act of sibling empathy, started crying and tried to crawl over Miss Marlo to get to me. She flattened him with a light karate chop to the back. He fell silent for a few seconds and then let out a freight train of a scream. The church stopped staring at us and turned to the ladies in white. *Do something,* their looks said. *Their screams are drowning out the Holy Ghost!*

"Breathe deep, honey," one of the ladies in white instructed me. As I opened my mouth to take in a big gasp of air, another lady in white popped a peppermint in my mouth.

"You can't give her those candies!" the first lady admonished. "They're for Sister Jean, in case she goes into diabetic shock!" The peppermint lady ignored her and started cooling my face with a funeral hand fan.

The service had completely stopped. Miss Marlo hugged my brother, who was slobbering on her shirt. "I'm so sorry," Miss Marlo whispered to the woman fanning me. "They've never been to a black church before." The woman glanced at Miss Marlo quizzically, put a cold towel on my head, and started singing about "a wretch like me."

I think my mother liked having a few hours during the weekend to herself, because she started buying me dresses so I could attend church with Miss Marlo every Sunday. The more I went, the more I became accustomed to Holy Ghost catching; actually, I welcomed it as an entertaining diversion from the three-hour-long church service.

About three months later, my mother announced that staying close to God was becoming a little too expensive. She couldn't handle having two kids in Catholic school and fulfill Baptist church dress-buying requirements. I was staying in Baptist church, but I was going to a public school.

"You'll like it. It's a magnet school for smart kids from all over the city," my mother said.

Public school? Kids from all over the city? That means all types of religions, I thought. I got excited thinking of opportunities to find a friend with a new religious community I could join.

Public school also meant public transportation—two buses

and the subway. It was my first time alone on public transportation, and on the first bus I was too intimidated by the crowd to claw my way off at my stop. I ended up having to walk over a mile back to the second bus stop, where two buses passed me by because I wasn't standing close enough to the curb. By the time I arrived at the school auditorium, I was bushed. I dragged myself into the assembly room and sat alone near a group of white kids.

There were more kids in the assembly room than I had ever seen in my entire life, and they all seemed to know one another. Some were chasing around; others were doing graffiti on notepads. None looked especially gifted to me.

A chubby white girl clutching a Trapper Keeper entered the auditorium looking just as overwhelmed as I did. She sat next to me and introduced herself. By seventh period, Dara Silberstein was my best friend.

Dara was a transfer from Hebrew school and glad to be in public school. When she talked about how much she hated Hebrew school, I shook my head like I knew what Hebrew school was. I thought being at a school for smart kids meant you had to know everything. I imagined if a teacher overheard me admitting ignorance of Hebrew school, she would call a hall monitor to escort me out through a secret dunce-cap-shaped door.

The second week of my new Best Friendship, I admitted to Dara that I was ignorant of all things Jewish. I explained that, in Catholic school, Jewish culture was next to Darwinism on the "things God really doesn't want us to talk about" list. Dara invited me to her house to spend the night and go to a synagogue.

I was hooked on Judaism halfway through the service. It combined the best of Catholic church (central air!) and Baptist church (talks of "how far we'd come since slavery"!) and had one important extra: No one passed around a collection plate. I figured the last part would appeal to my financially stressed mother and I'd be rewarded for finding a place to worship and save money simultaneously. I imagined how cute my brother would look in a beanie.

On the way back to Dara's house, I told her mother my Jewish desires.

Dara gasped and tried to warn me off the kosher path. "You'd have to leave and go to Hebrew school!"

Exactly, Dara. I wanted to go to Hebrew school. There, I planned to mix and mingle with Jewish children my age—my community.

"How cool would it be if you were Jewish!" Dara said, grabbing both of my hands and smiling. Her mother said nothing.

When my mother rang Dara's bell later that evening, I pounced on her before she stepped into the living room.

"Mom, can we be Jewish? Please?"

"Well, hello to you, too!" my mother said.

"Sorry. Hi, mom. Black people can be Jewish," I explained. I considered myself an expert on the subject, since I'd seen one black woman at the temple, sitting in the front row.

"Sing the song," Dara said, nudging me.

"Ain kaolhain no!" I sang out, doing my best version of the Hebrew chant that I had heard earlier. I remembered the words because the first line sounded like *ain't constipated.* To this day, I feel comfortable in any temple, because I still remember that first line.

My mom's eyebrows raised and her eyes widened; she stared at me as I belted out song after song in broken Hebrew.

"Yes, we've had quite a day," Dara's mother said. "Is Angela's father Jewish?" I've always wondered if she asked this because of the high percentage of Jewish males who hooked up with black women during the civil rights movement and gave birth to little Lenny Kravitzes.

My mom started choking on her juice. She beat her chest to clear her lungs and announced that it was time to go.

For months, I stuck to my Jewish plans. In my mind, I *was* Jewish. When Jehovah's Witnesses came to our door, I told them I was Jewish. I asked the lunch ladies if the tater tots were kosher. I used Yiddish terms Dara taught me in general conversations. This did not go over well at Miss Lillian's beauty salon.

"Mazel tov, shiksas!" I announced when entering the salon.

"What's with the Jewish thing?" Miss Lillian asked.

"You know the K on their bread stands for KKK, right?" Miss Marlo asked, after I politely refused a sandwich made on non-kosher bread.

"It's just a phase," my mother told them.

"No, it's not! They are my people! They have their own school and their own language. It's like a club," I replied.

"Well, for your sake, it'd better be a nice club because being black *and* Jewish you won't be able to get into any other ones," Miss Lillian informed me.

The next weekend, my mother decided to take me to a real club full of people like me, a multiracial group of parents and children entitled Rainbow Connections. (It wasn't that much of a rainbow; my mother was the only black mother there.)

I played board games with a new mixed friend while my mother sat uncomfortably in the back of the room listening to white women chatting excitedly about the upcoming Kwanzaa holiday.

When we got into the car to leave, my mother thumbed through the introduction brochure. On the cover, there was a cartoon WELCOME BIRACIAL PARENTS! banner with six happy light-brown children standing under it.

"I'm looking for meat-and-potatoes talk and they're serving up chips and soda," my mother said, scanning the last page. "If those people think their mixed children aren't black, they've got a rude awakening headed their way." She tossed the pamphlet into the backseat where, after two weeks of lying abandoned in the hot sun, the brown cartoon children faded to white.

A few weeks later, as she was cleaning out her car, she found the brochure and laughed.

"You know what? You and me, we can be our own club." She ripped up the faded children and replaced them with a Bible and a piece of kente cloth that sit in her car window to this day.

Fat Pam Is Real Black

"In America, which I love from the depths of my heart and soul, when you look like me, you're black."
—*Colin Powell*

My mother won't come out of pocket for anything unless it meets two conditions: high quality and low price. That's all fine when you're searching thrift-store racks for clothes, but a hard combination to find when you're hiring an overnight babysitter.

Betty, our first sitter, didn't like how watching two kids put a damper on her social life. Every weekend night, she'd drop my brother off with her cousin and take me out clubbing with her. Thanks to my steady diet of hormone-infused fast-food burgers, all it took was a low-cut top and some bright red lipstick to transform me from twelve to twenty-one.

Unfortunately, one morning my mother noticed the Club Passions VIP stamp on the back of my pubescent hand. She promptly fired Betty and walked me to the beauty salon, to see if anyone needed a babysitting gig.

"Fat Pam can watch her," a fellow customer, Miss Cheryl, offered.

Miss Cheryl was Fat Pam's mother. Like everyone else, Miss Cheryl called her daughter by her neighborhood name, so my mother wouldn't confuse her with Booster Pam, the woman who would steal anything you wanted if you paid her half the item's retail price.

My mother was sold on Fat Pam; she had a reputation around the beauty shop as a sweet, quiet girl. She wasn't running the streets like some nineteen-year-olds; she had a steady man she was going to marry when she was done with community college. Fat Pam would also watch us for only $75 a week.

My brother and I soon discovered that Pam was sweet and quiet only after she smoked a bag of weed. Sometimes, she wasn't even sweet and quiet then. If our upstairs neighbor was making too much noise while Pam was trying to relax in a weed-induced high, she'd make me and my brother chant "You're fucking up my high!" while hitting the ceiling with brooms and mops. It was the most fun game Fat Pam ever played with us.

When she wasn't high, she was Mean Pam. She was loud, she cursed like she was raised in a cell block, and she was quick to pick a fight, knowing that no one wanted to take on a three-hundred-pound woman. Mean Pam saw it as her job not only to babysit me but also to use her weight and her mouth to bully me into being a Real Black Person.

Pam's Real Black Person Rules

Real Black People's hair should be bone-straight or in a Jeri-Curl, no matter how many chemical burns it takes to get that way.

Real Black People accessorize with gold jewelry. The more jewelry men have, the more you should flirt with them. Women should have big gold hoop earrings to attract the men with the gold jewelry. If you can't afford real gold, buy some fake earrings from a Chinese vendor and coat them in clear nail polish so they won't turn green.

Real Black People never, ever listen to white music unless George Michael sings it.

Real Black People should know at least one break-dancing move.

Real Black People know how to fight.

Real Black People wear clean clothes and name-brand sneakers. If your sneakers get scuffed, you should throw them out.

Real Black People do not have white best friends.

"Like, omigod, it's your friend Dara, like, on the phone," Pam said, using her best imitation of a white-girl voice.

"Why is a white girl your best friend?" she asked me, after her intense staring forced me to cut my conversation with Dara short.

"Because she is," I replied. I felt safe giving a flippant response. Pam had already smoked three joints and was floating on a cloud of drug tranquillity.

"You know you're black, right?" Pam asked me, her tone implying that I didn't. "If you don't know now, you're going to know when I get done with you."

Pam's community college was across the street from my school, which meant I had to endure two buses and a subway's worth of Real Black Person notes.

"Real Black People use laundry tokens instead of subway tokens to pay the bus fare," Pam said, before pocketing the money my mother had given me and slipping a Laundromat token into the fare box.

"C'mon, let's go to the back," Pam called out, once we were on the bus. "Real Black People sit in the back."

When Pam walked me to school, she took great pains to point out people who were blacker than I was.

"See, she's a Real Black Person," Pam said, pointing to Tascha, a girl who sucked her teeth every time she saw me in the hallway. According to Tascha, I was a "light-skinned bitch." At least, that's what she called out to me a few times after sucking her teeth.

. . .

"Christina don't like you either," Tascha informed me, interrupting my walk from Science to Home Economics. "She says you be grittin' on her too much," Tascha continued, before she turned away from me and headed down the hall. "You do be grittin' on people too hard," she yelled over her shoulder. Of course, all the boys were looking when she said this. When Tascha walked, every male in the building stared, their eyes stuck on her perfect ass until the wavy logo of her Lee jeans back pockets turned the corner.

Christina and Tascha were unlike any girls I'd ever met. They were fourteen going on twenty-four. They went to Planned Parenthood after school and showed off their birth control pills in the cafeteria. They'd complain between classes about how most of the other black students at our school were childish and corny. If it was raining, I knew Tascha and Christina would show up with plastic caps and curlers so not one drop of water would mess up their sexy asymmetrical haircuts. I peered over their shoulders as they compared their Liz Claiborne purses and their gold name earrings and passed notes in their girly bubblescript handwriting. They always dotted their i's with hearts. So yes, one could say I was grittin' on Christina and Tascha, but it was with intrigue and admiration, the way you would stare at a celebrity.

"I told you black people don't like to be stared at. You better watch out, they're probably going to jump you," Pam nonchalantly warned me after I asked her to check her Real Black Dictionary and tell me what *gritting* meant.

The knowledge that I was on the verge of getting my ass kicked only made me stare harder. I figured I had a reason to stare: I had to see if they were gearing up to slaughter me. I refused to get jumped unexpectedly.

I tried to delay the beatdown Pam predicted by becoming Christina and Tascha's unwanted helper. I'd get in the dessert line at school, even though I didn't want dessert; I wanted to call out

Christina's name when I hit the head of the line so she could get in front of me. I let Tascha borrow anything of mine she needed: my homework, my allowance, my gloves. Unfortunately, pushing myself on the girls only gave them more time to study me and find new things to hate.

"You talk white," Christina said, after I let her borrow all my birthday money.

"She dresses white, too," someone else yelled out.

"Why don't you get a new hairstyle? You look like a DeBarge reject!" Tascha said, after I bought her Doritos.

If I'd known in eighth grade what I know now, I would have said, "Thank you, see you in twenty years, when you're sitting with your ten kids and your biggest accomplishment was telling someone she talks white." Maybe I'd have rejoined Dara at her table or at least saddled up with some of the "corny" black kids. I don't know why I had this relentless drive to please my bullies. Perhaps it was because I was younger than everyone else and my mind wasn't developed enough not to care what people thought; more likely it was because I was just doing what I could to keep the peace in one part of my life. Between Pam at home and the cool clique in school, all that teasing was wearing me down.

Pam instructed me that the way out of being teased was to vigorously study her Real Black People lessons.

"You have to learn to dance, learn to fight, and get some white Reebok high-top sneakers," Pam instructed me, throwing away my supermarket loafers. The way Pam said it, white high-top Reeboks would be my talisman; once I secured a pair, I'd get the respect of Christina and Tascha. "Whatever you got to do to get your mom to buy them, do it," Pam said. I knew I had to lie; my mother would rather bring George Bush as a date to her Black Panther reunion than buy name-brand sneakers.

I told my mother that high-top Reeboks were a Physical Education requirement. "Mr. Greer said I'll break my ankle if I have the cheap shoes," I said. My mom eyed me suspiciously, then told me to get in the car. "I have to see these special ankle-protecting sneakers," she said when we pulled up to Foot Hut, our local Foot Locker knockoff.

"Fifty dollars? What are these shoes made of, gold?" my mother yelled out to the salesman, dropping the sample shoe like it was burning her hand. "Fifty dollars for sneakers? Do you know what I could do with fifty dollars?" she asked me.

"Buy me those sneakers so I won't break my ankles?" I asked, knowing, of course, that wasn't the right answer.

"How about I write Mr. Greer a note and tell him that my boss doesn't pay me Reebok money. I'll tell him I work in a hospital, so I can get you an ankle cast for free."

We left Foot Hut and went down the street to Fayva, where we purchased their version of Reebok high-tops. "They look just like Reeboks," my mother said. They did, except BALLOONS was stitched into the side where the Reebok logo was on the real high-tops. I knew going to school with fake Reeboks would be worse than going to school with no sneakers at all, so I spent two hours in my room using Wite-Out to carefully cover each letter of BALLOONS. When it dried, I took a thin black marker and stenciled REEBOK on top of the Wite-Out.

The next day, I proudly stomped my "Reeboks" through seven periods. *Look at me—I'm really black!* Every move I made was a ballet move; I didn't turn corners, I pirouetted, raising my calf off the floor and rotating 90 degrees to make sure everyone caught a glimpse of my sneakers. The eighth and final period of the day, I shifted in my seat and jutted my legs out into the aisle so that Fred, a male member of the cool black clique, could have an unobstructed view of my feet.

"Look at her sneakers!" Fred whispered to Christina when our teacher, Mrs. Bratspir, was stuck on the wall phone, taking a note from the office.

Christina looked at my feet, and a shotgun blast of laughter burst out of her mouth.

As handy as Wite-Out is, it isn't made for large-scale projects like sneaker copyright infringement. When I looked down to see what they were laughing at, I saw that I now had BALLBOKS instead of REEBOKS. Half of my Wite-Out had rubbed off, leaving the first half of the BALLOONS logo to merge with my handwritten BOK. Having Ballboks was even worse than having Balloons: to seventh-graders, any punch line that contained the word *ball* was deemed twenty times funnier than one without a phallic reference.

"Ballbok!" Fred sputtered out. He dropped over his desk, shaking it as the laughter overtook his entire body.

Mrs. Bratspir covered the receiver of the wall phone and turned to Fred, her eyes blazing black. "Are you insane?" she asked.

"Ballbok!" Fred screamed out and pointed at my shoes.

Mrs. Bratspir hung up the phone and walked slowly toward Fred's pointing finger. It was the only time in three years of being her student that I ever heard her laugh. She looked at me with pity and amusement, shook her head, and began the lesson on DNA.

The Ballboks let everyone know that I knew I wasn't cool and, more important, that I cared. Now I was not only uncool with the popular kids, I was also shunned by the nerds.

The bullying at school worsened. Tascha would threaten to cut my hair in the cafeteria, Christina would force girls to throw me against my locker while I was trying to open it. Several times I left school with red marks and dents on my face. I couldn't eat, I had knots of fear in my stomach. Every day, I'd hear a new rumor about when I was going to get my ass kicked. When school let out, I'd either hide until Christina and Tascha left or run as fast as I could to the subway, hopping on it before the girls arrived.

I felt I had no one to turn to. I had abandoned Dara when both Pam and the cool kids had made fun of our friendship. I tried to go back to her, but it was awkward. She was into boys, so she tried to hook me up, but none of the white guys found me attractive. I played lookout for a short time, while she kissed her boyfriend during recess, but soon that made me feel even lonelier than when I sat by myself.

I rationalized that I couldn't tell my teachers; what could they do, walk me to the subway every day? Plus, Christina and Tascha would kill me if they found out I'd told. I decided that Pam, being a Real Black Person, could teach me how to fight. Pam owed me at least a fighting lesson. Besides being her usual mean self, she'd begun lying to people and telling them I was her daughter. According to Pam, having a half-white daughter would up her status with black people.

While shopping, we ran into a friend she hadn't seen since junior high.

"Are these your kids?" her friend asked.

"Yeah, these are my little brats," she said, looking at my brother and me, daring us to contradict her.

"You got with a white man?" her friend asked. Pam smiled and nodded her head up and down. On the spot, she made up a well-detailed lie about her babies' rich Italian father.

"Ooh, I can't wait until she spreads that around! I'm gonna be just like Diana Ross. She ain't the only bitch can have a white husband," she explained to me, before we walked to the corner store to buy a night's worth of marijuana.

When I asked Pam for boxing lessons, she seemed proud, like a mother bird watching her chick preparing to take a solo flight. She stood up and put her fists against her cheeks. "Protect your face," she instructed me. "When I fight light-skinned girls, I always go for the face."

The next day, Tascha pushed me against my locker, leaving a long scratch on my cheek. I was too afraid to push her back. When Pam saw the scratch, she pronounced me untrainable. "You don't have the heart," she said. "That's your white side."

I stuck to my original plan of waiting ten minutes before leaving school. One day, Christina and Tascha decided to wait for me underground. I tensed up as they approached me. Christina ripped my schoolbag from my back and threw it on the train tracks.

Tascha grabbed my arm and tried to swing me onto the tracks. I grabbed her, and in a violent tango, she ripped my shirt and I grabbed her hair. The other girls cheered Tascha on.

Several adults were watching. I hoped someone would jump in, but each time I caught someone's eye, they looked away.

I slammed my heel down on Tascha's sneaker. The pain of my cheap plastic heel on her Reeboks caused her to let go of me.

"What did I ever do to you?" I yelled, panting for air.

Christina pulled on Tascha's arm. "Leave her alone. She ain't worth getting expelled for."

I couldn't believe the same girls who had almost murdered me were actually worried about their academic careers. Thank God I have gifted school bullies, I thought.

"Stuck-up yellow bitch," another member of the crew yelled at me before they all walked to the other end of the platform. When the train arrived, I saw my book bag get blown to pieces. I folded my arms against my chest to cover up the hole in my shirt and got on the train.

When I arrived home, Pam was mad at me for losing my books. When she had me pick the seeds out of her marijuana bag that night, I saved some to show my mother. I cried as I handed them over later.

"Those are Pam's seeds," I said, and started crying.

"Oh, my goodness, I'm so sorry," my mother said. "No wonder all of my clothes smell like Black Love incense! I'll get rid of her, you don't have to cry."

"Please don't hire any more Real Black People! I hate black people!" I screamed, before running and locking myself in my room.

I didn't want to have a mother-daughter mulatto moment like the ones we had after the zebra teasings and the your-dad-isn't-white scuffles. I didn't want another race lesson or an analysis of how crazy everyone else was and how special I was. I wanted out of the race game. It seemed every time I learned the rules, someone changed them on me. I was tired of fighting. I wanted to be a purebred.

I grabbed my seventh-grade yearbook and studied the photos. Unlike my previous schools, there were a few people who had both my complexion and skin color: María, José, Blanca. I went to the mirror armed with two months of junior high Spanish and practiced my new identity.

"Mixed? No," I said, a frown on my face. *"Yo soy puertorriqueña!"* I said, and smiled.

Yellow Cab

With beauty, charm, sweetness of personality, the "correct" color and now an inheritance to boot, my mother had many suitors.

—Shirlee Taylor Haizlip, The Sweeter the Juice:
A Family Memoir in Black and White

Dear [insert rapper's name here]:

My name is Angela a.k.a. Lady A. I go to a gifted school and I love your rhymes. My dream is to get a recording contract and hear myself on the radio just like you. I have a beef with some girls at school because I'm light-skinned, but like you say in your rap: [insert verse about outdoing the competition], so I ain't even worried about it. Anyway, if you have time, could you come to my school and give a concert? My contact information is below.

I sent out at least one hundred of these letters. (God, I needed some friends!) The only time I deviated from that rapper form letter was when I had a massive crush on Cockroach (Theo's best friend) from *The Cosby Show* and wrote him a three-page letter complete with stickers. With the rappers, I honestly thought one was going to read my letter, blast into my junior high auditorium, grab the microphone, and be like, "Hey, Christina! Bullying is wack, so step back!" (or something like that).

Hell, it was 1988, so it could have happened. In '88 emcees

were rapping about all kinds of topics, very few of them gun-related. The most popular song on the air was "Picking Boogers," where the most offensive verse detailed how the rapper snuck "a little green one" into another rapper's spaghetti.

There wasn't a rap I didn't know, and that was a huge feat, because even though hip-hop was played for only two hours every night (it was considered street kiddie music, so even the black stations marketed themselves as having "rap-free workdays!"), there were hundreds of rappers. Every time someone came out with a hit song or group idea, someone else would come out with a follow-up. "Roxanne Roxanne" by UTFO had more than a hundred response records. The Fat Boys came out, and soon there was a group called the Skinny Boys. Run-D.M.C. came out with "My Adidas," and another group came out with "My Fila." You'd hear a song on the radio and it would sound like the guy from down the block, and it would turn out to *be* the guy from down the block. If you were a city kid in the eighties, you can understand why I felt I had a good chance of a rapper responding and personalizing an antibully rap for me.

Still, I wasn't going to sit around and wait for Biz Markie to show up at my school. I continued taping the rap show every single night, using other songs' beats to write my own rhymes. I'd use my curling iron as a microphone. I'd imagine all my bullies begging to get into my concert.

Two weeks into the summer of 1988, my hip-hop addiction gave me answers that no adult had. My bullies hate light-skinned girls because the boys love us!

Seriously, if you were a light-skinned girl in an all-black community, 1988 was a banner year for high self-esteem. The next time you encounter a thirty-something light-skinned woman with her head in the air, ask her what year her nose got stuck there. After she looks you up and down and inquires about the type of car you're driving, she'll undoubtedly reply, "Why, 1988, of course, the year of Light Power."

Forget being Puerto Rican, I thought. Because of rap, you'll finally be popular!

I made a mix tape of high-yellow hits. It started off with J.J. Fad rapping about being "light-skinned and devastating" and ended with Big Daddy Kane's declaration of love to women who looked like me.

MTV Raps premiered that year, and I watched with pride. The majority of the women in the videos had my complexion.

Dear God, I prayed, thank you for getting me out of the white neighborhood. I may have been ugly to them, but to black people, being light is almost as good as being white! Why didn't my mother tell me that when I cried about being next to last on the ugly list at Catholic school? Did she hate me, too? I wondered. Probably. Why else would my curfew still be when the streetlights come on? *I'm almost grown! I'm thirteen! I wear a bigger bra than she does! She's probably jealous of that, too.*

I changed my rap name from Lady A to Big Red, as in Big Red-bone, the nickname boys called light-skinned girls, even though no one knew what it meant. I'd rap *I'm light-skinned and devastatin'/all your men I will be takin'* into my curling iron. I'd pretend I was the only girl member of a rap crew. "She's light-skinned and devastating," my imaginary posse would chorus before posing in a b-boy stance as spotlights shone down and lit up my fly melanin-deficient self.

Being confident that I was in style like Adidas sneakers and Spuds MacKenzie, I was ready to take my new self-esteem show on the road. When I rode the bus in the morning, I now held boys' gazes instead of acting like I was fascinated by the above-seat ads. Most boys reacted to my attention by smiling and motioning me over with their index fingers. I'd mimic what the older girls did; I'd shake my head *no* and make the boys come to me.

Finding out that I was pretty was like being a starving dog and getting locked in a meat factory. I went crazy feeding my appetite. There were approximately 200,000 black boys in Philadelphia between the ages of thirteen and eighteen, and I tried to collect the whole set. I stacked up boyfriends like a cheerleading pyramid. There was Allen with the inverted widow's peak and the gigantic collection of baseball caps to cover it up. And William, who sometimes smelled like cat but he could draw his ass off and proclaimed his love for me in big graffiti bubble letters on the side of a pizza parlor wall: Will ♥ Big Red.

Some members of my stable were simply guys that other girls wanted, like the light-skinned boys that favored Al B. Sure!, the popular R and B singer of the day. Some were guys that no one wanted but I took on because, hey, you never know when your book bag might need carrying.

There was one type of guy that could make me get rid of all of the others: a guy with a car. This was not because I was a mini gold digger (not yet), but because a car guaranteed a way for me to zoom away from danger at the end of the school day. Goodbye, Christina! Goodbye, Tascha! Those girls could say they were going to kick my ass even more for being a ho, but they'd have to say it to the tailpipe. *Vrooom! Beep beep!*

I didn't need to be funny or smart, just tan. Lots of times, boys would compliment my complexion as their opening pickup line. "Y'all light-skinned girls are just so pretty," some would say. I didn't care that they felt that way for the same reason they wore gold rope chains and Jordan sneakers—because Big Daddy Kane did.

I became even more secure in my light skin when I discovered the mania was deeper than life imitating hip-hop. Sometimes, one of my boyfriends' hip-hop-hating mothers would coo out, "I knew he'd bring home a pretty high-yellow girl," or "Oooh, y'all going to have some pretty light babies!" I'd smile, getting an award for something I had nothing to do with.

Still, for every mother who loved me before I even opened my mouth, there were older versions of Christina who threw me shade for no reason. Will, a boyfriend I considered serious because we had been seeing each other for almost a whole month (and I only had one other boyfriend besides him), straight up told me that his mom didn't like light-skinned people, especially women. If he hadn't told me, I would have figured it out for myself. Every time I went over, she'd grunt out a hello and say nothing else, even if I tried to initiate a conversation with her. Did she know how many fake girlfriends I had to invent to even get out of the house to see her son? I thought I could win her over, even going so far as to plan to get a photo of me and my mother airbrushed on my jean jacket so she could see I came from dark-skinned stock.

One night, Will and I were driving home from the movies. We had started going to the movies in the suburbs because our regular haunt downtown had become a haven for bootleggers who would get mad at people for laughing ("Shut up, I'm taping, yo!")

We were debating whether a family could actually leave their kid home alone when a police cruiser pulled behind us and followed us for more than a mile. My fears shifted from how I was going to hide my hickey from my mother to whether I was going to jail. Since some members of my boy pyramid had bad reputations, Miss Marlo had taken me on a tour of local juvenile halls, hoping to scare me straight. I lounged in the backseat of her car trying to look disinterested while thinking that I could survive in an all-girl gang. At the least, I'd make some tough girlfriends in jail and we'd all go back and kick the asses of everyone who'd put me there.

Will was not one of the bad boys, he was a young black man driving in a late-model car down a white suburban street. "Why are they messing with me?" he said, his good-guy hands nervously clutching the steering. Un-street-smart girl that I was, I turned around to look at the police car.

"Don't look back! That'll make them stop us!" Will reprimanded me.

Sure enough, the police car's red and blue lights flickered on and Will pulled over. One officer approached my door and silently aimed his flashlight on the ignition. Will jingled his keys nonchalantly to show the officer that the car was not hotwired. By the time the cop on Will's side asked for his license and registration, four more police cars had come screeching up with their lights on, sirens blaring.

"Can I ask what I'm being stopped for, officer?" Will asked.

"There was a robbery in the area," the cop responded, his eyes scanning me and the rest of the car's interior. He was lying. I could just tell (it also didn't hurt that the only black officer there put her gun down and rolled her eyes when she heard him). I wondered if the next thing out of the cop's mouth wasn't going to be that the supposed assailants committed the robbery with the brick-sized Kit Kat sitting on the dashboard, left over from the movie.

A string of cars, mostly full of white people returning to their suburban homes, slowed down to stare at us. They were probably wondering if the house we'd broken into was near theirs; surely, that was what warranted the four cop cars surrounding us.

"Shit, he's probably going to plant some drugs," Will said, and put his head in his hands after giving the officer permission to search the trunk. Guys often complained about cops doing that; I thought they were lying until I dated a cop who admitted to it, explaining that he had forty-eight hours to turn over evidence taken from a crime scene and sometimes kept a small stash just to bust someone with. "It's frustrating to catch someone you know is selling drugs and not find anything," he said, explaining to me that I'd only understand if I was a cop.

Luckily for Will and me, there was no plant. After a half hour, we were sent on our way with "better safe than sorry" and "go straight home." *Why? So we don't get stopped again?* We took heed of the officer's words, but only because Will was pissed. As soon as he hit his mom's door, he unleashed and screamed out to his mom what happened. He wasn't mad that they'd stopped him. If they'd stopped only him, he'd be fine, he said. It was that they ruined our date.

Will's mom was watching television and seemed concerned until he mentioned the date. Then she went back to watching television, saying, "Oh, well, you shouldn't be riding through the suburbs with her light ass. That white cop probably thought you were with a white girl. That's why he stopped you."

I was crushed. I thought I was a part of the "driving while black" experience that had just happened—a victim, even—but apparently I'd caused it. Who did I think I was, being high yellow at night on a suburban street? How could I not know that such a combination would bring the black man down?

Will stepped between his mother and the television. Lord, don't let any fighting start, I thought. I can't even fight the girls at school, so I know I'm not prepared to swing on anyone's mother.

"Will, just take me home, it's okay," I said, grabbing his arm.

"He's not taking you nowhere, that's my car," his mom said, still not looking away from the television set. "Don't ever get somewhere you can't get home from."

Will got permission to walk me to the subway. We knew it was over for us. I was more pissed than heartbroken, pissed that his mother had decided for us. Pissed that he couldn't be some urban Romeo and choose me over his family. When I hopped off the subway and saw I'd missed the last bus home, I was pissed for being so dumb as to give up my other guys with cars for Will.

I headed to the phone booth and pulled out my little black book. I started calling guys I hadn't talked to in months in search of a ride home. I was only three names into the A's when I reached someone.

"Hey, Ali, I need a ride home," I said, using my sexiest desperate teenage voice.

"Who's this?"

"It's Angie," I said.

"Light-skinned Angie?"

"Yeah," I said.

I heard him pick up his keys. "I'll be right there."

Too Black, Too Poor

Like any American group achieving contemporary middle class station, black entrée into the culture of consumption made status an obsession and addiction to simulate a way of life.

—*Cornel West*, Race Matters

At the beginning of ninth grade, my mother decided to move us to an all-black middle-class neighborhood on the edge of Philadelphia.

Our new block was full of conspicuous-consumption-minded colored folks; it was a showcase of late-model cars and high-end above-ground pools. Some homeowners went a step further, erecting columns and faux-marble lions to guard their row homes.

"I remember when this used to be swampland," my grandmother said as she limped up the steps to our new rental house. "Now it's uppity-Negro land."

My neighborhood was known to most of my black schoolmates as "the Black Boonies" or "the Coonies." Few students admitted living there, instead claiming the vaguer "Southwest Philly" as their home base. To admit you were from the Black Boonies could make you a target: kids from tougher neighborhoods assumed that you were weak and your family had lots of money.

Most Boonie households actually didn't have a lot of money. The adults held government jobs and put in truckloads of overtime to pay for their lion statues.

Right away, I could tell we weren't going to fit in. We were the only single-parent family, we were the only people with mismatched hubcaps on our car, and, as we heard through the fast-moving neighborhood grapevine, we were the only (gasp!) renters.

"I know your landlord," Doison, an older girl who lived on the corner, told me, after my mother prodded me to go outside and make friends. "Did your landlord tell you that an eighty-year-old white lady died in your house?"

What was I supposed to say to that? My landlord had told me nothing; in fact, no one in our family had actually met the man. All I knew was he was African and the transaction was done entirely through his white girlfriend, who worked at the hospital with my mother. From what I'd gathered through eavesdropping, the white girlfriend and my mother were kinda "interracial couples" buddies and the white lady convinced her African boyfriend to rent us the house at the lowest rate he could afford. It was our first and only instance of interracial affirmative action.

"I was there the day the coroner carried her out. Her hand was all pale and it fell out from the bag and everyone screamed—"

"Doison!" her mom exclaimed, embarrassed. "You don't tell someone that about their house!"

Doison's mom was in her post office uniform, looking up into her front tree as she ran a broom through its leaves.

"Got it!" Doison's mom yelled, and I watched in horror as a nest holding two hairless baby birds dropped to the ground. Doison's mom then grabbed the hose from her garage and power-sprayed the nest and the baby birds into the sewer. Having completed her murder, she pumped her fists in the air and shouted, "That's what y'all get for pooping on my coupe!"

She then turned to me. "Welcome to the neighborhood."

"Nice to meet you," I lied, before running in to tell my mother the crazy shit I'd just witnessed.

"That's disgusting," my mother said. "I'll never understand how people can love their cars more than living creatures. As long as a car gets you where you're going and back, that's all you need."

The next day, as if God was testing her on that statement, our Ford Granada conked out while my mother was driving home from work. To replace it, she bought a nineteen-year-old Chevy Nova for $125 from the Pennysaver. The Nova's floor was rusted through, and the roof and front window leaked when it rained. Somebody must have paid a mechanic off because it had passed state inspection. It did not, however, pass the muster of our block. Doison and the other kids would yell out the names of cars and other items they'd be less embarrassed to be seen in whenever my mother chugged down the block. "I'd rather drive a lawn mower!" "A Yugo!" "A donkey!"

Because of the car's leaky front window, my mother often had to wear a rain bonnet while driving, and my brother and I had to ride together in the backseat. To avoid watching Doison make fun of us, my brother and I would dive to the floor of the backseat whenever we reached our neighborhood. The more we hid, the angrier my mother became. "If you don't like my car, you can get out and walk!" My brother and I would look at each other, crouched on the dirty floor of the Nova. *Is she serious? Because if she is, I'd really rather walk.*

Luckily, yelling out our car's inadequacies was as rough as it would get in that hood. Our neighbors viewed themselves as urban sophisticates, and fighting was for poor people—more precisely, niggas. That neighborhood was the first time I heard the word *nigga* used by black people derogatorily about other black people. Until then, my friends and I used the word as a synonym for "close male friend" (as in "That's my nigga!"). Now a nigga was a lower-class black person that good hardworking black people had nothing in common with—the people formerly known as Real Black People.

Oh, how I wished my mother could be a nigga just for a second. I wanted her to pop one of those "Yugo" screamers square in the jaw. My mother only wanted to keep the peace: just ride in her Nova, feed her kids, and pay her bills. Even when some women on the block gossiped that she'd moved to the block looking for a husband to steal (what else would a single woman with kids be trying to do?), she didn't confront anyone. The next rumor was that she was on welfare (look at her car, plus how could a woman on her own afford the rent on that house?), but she shook that one off, too.

"Some black people are like crabs in a barrel," she explained. "As soon as they see one doing well, they'll pull him down." To me, it sounded like being a crab was worse than being a nigga.

My mom hadn't moved us to the all-black Boonies to teach me about crabs or niggas; she says it was simply to get us out of a small apartment and into a house. I do wonder if she moved us to that neighborhood because she knew it would cause my fear of black girls to disappear. There was no way to hate black girls when you lived in an all-black neighborhood; if I did, I'd be hating a lot of people who looked awfully similar to me. At least half of the people in my neighborhood had my complexion, and since my mother had decided that I was old enough for a relaxer, my hair was now bone straight and no longer stuck out as "good." No one ever asked me if I was biracial and I never thought about it. I read an article in one of my mother's *Ebony* magazines detailing how 90 percent of black people have European ancestry. I just have a little more than most black people, I deduced.

I came to view white people as the rest of the people in our neighborhood did. They took on this kind of city health inspector quality; we always had to be clean and on our best behavior in case they showed up. If girls on the street started to argue too loudly or if someone went outside with wrinkled clothes, the favored parental admonishment was, "You're acting just like white people want you to act. They'll say, *See, those black people live in a nice part of town and still act the fool!*" Kids fell in line quickly when an adult said that. The thought of a white person looking down on them was more terrifying than a month's worth of punishment.

· · ·

About a year after we moved, I was forced to remember exactly how much European blood I had

"Would you believe Urban invited us to Diane's wedding?" my mother asked me.

Huh? Who invited us where?

"Your paternal grandfather. I haven't spoken to that side of the family in years. I think it would be rude not to go, though."

At the time, one quarter of my hair was shaved almost bald like that of my newest favorite rapper, MC Lyte. The short area always had designs etched in it, courtesy of a barbershop's clippers. My mom begged me to let my latest design (the word *def*) grow out before we saw our white relatives.

My brother asked if my father would be there. My mother said his sister disliked him and left it at that. I figured I really had to be on my best behavior around these white people. If one cut off their own brother from coming to a wedding, they'd sure cut my black ass off at the slightest infraction.

After two hours on some roads I am certain no black people have ever traveled before, we arrived at the church right on time. When we came through the church doors, half the wedding party gasped and clutched their hearts like we were Jesus himself walking on water and into their church. I wanted to run out. I pulled on my mother's arm like I was a little girl. "Just walk in," she said, through clenched smiling teeth, trying to kill everyone with the kindness that was shooting out of her eyes. I grabbed my brother's hand, something I was way too cool to do in Philly. I figured, if we were getting lynched, we'd go down as a family.

During the ceremony, I sat uncomfortably close to my mother. She gave surreptitious glances toward unrecognizable faces. "That's your cousin," she whispered, pointing to a red-haired boy about my age in the front row. "You met him when you were four." I didn't remember any of them and felt no connection.

After the ceremony, my grandfather shouted, "There's my granddaughter!" and came running over to me with outstretched arms. I was glad he knew who I was because I couldn't remember what he looked like and would have hugged and kissed any white man over sixty if my mother had told me he was my grandfather.

"That's wild!" he said, and I politely thanked my grandfather for the "wild!" He was too loud, the attention felt forced, like he was doing it for other people. If he was so happy to see me, why hadn't he called me in years?

As I spun around, showing my grandfather the layers of my hairdo, I saw my aunt's new husband's eyes widen in shock. It reminded me of all the hateful stares from my childhood pasta-gathering missions. When my aunt introduced us to our new uncle, he gave me a stiff hug with a pat on the back. For the first time since I'd moved to the Boonies, I wished I was whiter. Not only so I wouldn't stick out, but so I wouldn't make the groom, one of the most important people of the day, uncomfortable. I felt offensive in my own skin.

The reception was in the basement of the church, and I kept drinking water so I wouldn't have to talk to anyone. Of course, with all that water, I had to find the ladies' room, but I was afraid to go alone. I held it in, shaking, until my mother got up to go, too.

When we walked in, the bathroom went silent. Women know when someone's been talking about them, and both my mother and myself knew we had just been on people's lips. Refusing to stoop to their level, my mother smiled again and went into the only open stall.

"So, Janice, which one married the colored lady? Is he here?" came a voice from the stall next to my mother's, that of a woman in the middle of a long pee, unaware that the colored lady had entered.

"I married Jack, Urban's son," my mother replied over the stall. The room fell silent for a moment, followed by a rush of toilet flushes, closing compacts, and high heels clicking out the door across the linoleum.

My mom was obviously shaken. She called me into her stall because she couldn't steady her hand to pin her slip back on to her skirt (the slip's elastic had given out over a year ago and she didn't find it necessary to splurge on a new slip when safety pins worked just as well). After I secured the slip to her skirt, we walked back out, just in time to throw some rice at the bride and groom.

My mom was totally composed when we hit the church steps. With her head poised like an Ethiopian queen, she grabbed a handful of rice and pulled back her arm slowly and dramatically, like an Alvin Ailey dancer. When she threw the rice, she overextended her reach. We heard a rip. Her skirt dropped to the ground, taking her attached slip with it.

With all the white faces staring and nothing but her panties and control-top hose covering her bottom half, my mother grabbed her clothes and jumped behind some bushes to cover herself.

I felt horrible for my mother, but I had never seen anything funnier in my life. Tears shot out from my eyes while I convulsed trying to hold my laughs in. I knew not to laugh too hard in front of the white people. *Be on your best behavior.*

While my mother wriggled her way back into her skirt behind the bushes, I pretended to be crying for the bride and groom. While dabbing at my eyes with a napkin, I wondered if acting good for the white folks at this point really made any difference. Was there any coming back from the half-naked black woman who jumped into a bush?

"Never again," my mother said as we got into the car. My white relatives must have said the same thing, because we never saw or talked to any of them after that. Other than my father, I have no idea to this day what any of my white relatives look like.

After two hours of driving, we reached the edge of our neighborhood. When my brother and I crouched, as usual, on the floor of the car, my mother went off.

"After all we've been through today? Are you ashamed of me? If you don't get up by the time we hit our block, you can both get your ungrateful butts out and walk!" my mother yelled at us through the rearview mirror. J.R. and I looked at each other, and for a second we felt really badly. Then, as soon as Mom came to a stop sign, I tried to take her up on her walking offer and pushed the rear door open, but the entire thing fell off, rusted from the hinges by recent rains. It sounded like a jackhammer as it hit the concrete.

"Oooh!" my brother yelled and pointed to me, as if it wasn't obvious to my mother that the kid *outside* the car was the one who had broken the door.

Instant karma is a bitch. I had to help my mother lift the door and push it into the backseat of the car and then sit on top of it as we rode down the block. Doison led the block in a group rendition of the *Sanford and Son* theme as we pulled into our driveway.

"It's good to be home," my mother said, ignoring the laughing children as she held her dress together and skipped up the front steps.

Two Longer Bus Rides
and a Benz

Diversity rocks!

—Classmate's signature in my
tenth-grade yearbook

By the middle of ninth grade, I had a cumulative C grade average. Two and a half years of cutting classes to avoid bullies and then not raising my hand when I was in class (to avoid being labeled as "acting white") had caught up to me.

Okay, spending every night on the phone with my boyfriends instead of doing homework didn't help either.

Anyway, I applied to, and was summarily rejected from, all of the top-tier magnet schools. I received one acceptance letter, from a small agricultural school. "We welcome you, future farmer!" the letter began. The only other option I had was the neighborhood high school, which had recently installed metal detectors. ("I'll work as a hooker and home-school you before I let you go there," my mother said.)

As exciting as it would have been to pick my mother up from the strip every night, I told her my choice was the agricultural high school.

"Mom, I can't fail at farm school because black people are more in touch with nature," I said, putting a cassette in my boom box. "It says so right here in this song," I continued, turning the volume up.

A short blip of black pride had fallen over hip-hop and even though I mourned the end of the light-skinned era, I was hooked. I was learning more listening to the radio than I was in my classes. The top song was KRS-ONE's "You Must Learn," in which he rapped about black inventors. A black man invented the traffic light? Pioneered the first blood bank? How come I hadn't learned this in school? Before that song, the only black inventor I knew was the peanut butter guy. As cool as peanut butter is, it's a bit shameful for that to be the crowning achievement of your race.

"Mom, school isn't meant for black people. If it is, how come they don't teach about anyone except Martin Luther King?" I asked, hoping to tap into her latent Black Panther.

"Maybe they covered it on the day you were cutting," she replied.

I decided that I'd just cruise through agricultural school and spend my free time concentrating on a rap career, though I didn't quite know where I fit in with the conscious rap movement. For example, I could never mention my brother's name around hip-hop heads. *Jack* was now the official name for *the white man*, thanks to Public Enemy. To tell someone you had a black brother named Jack would be like telling someone you had a black brother named Honky. "Why on earth would your mom name a black man Jack?" people would ask me. "It's his dad's name," I'd say, like we had different dads.

Some people took the pro-black hip-hop movement as a chance for retribution against all the attention light-skinned people had been getting. It was already an accepted stereotype that light-skinned girls couldn't fight, but now some people were saying we weren't even all that pretty. One rapper had a moderate radio hit with "Dark-Skinned Girls," a song about how horrible and stuck-up girls of my hue were.

Once, while watching a made-for-TV movie, I caught a vision of my new rap marketing scheme. The television mother was explaining to her daughter that she had the family ability to see the future. "It's both a gift and a curse," the mother said. That's what I decided being light-skinned was. I decided my first album would be titled *Light-Skinned: The Gift and the Curse.* I wrote songs atoning for my past abundance of self-love and ones asserting that, even though I was light, I was still blacker than most people. Had a record label actually signed me, people would be laughing at the VH1 *Where Is She Now?* special featuring my hit "Your Mom Don't Like Light Skin" and "No Hot Sauce, Bitch," my requisite militant track, inspired by all the times waitresses assumed I wanted hot sauce because I was black.

My mother, of course, was beside herself with concern when I told her my career plans. I don't know which she thought was worse: that I'd actually become a rapper or that I'd excel at farm school and she'd have to introduce me as her daughter the sheepherder. A few days later, she told me she was going figure out how to get me into "a rich white private school where no one cares about rap," she said. "Hopefully, one without boys," she added.

All "rich white private schools" required a test given by an educational company before admittance. Part of the test was interactive: the administrator would say a string of numbers ("six, five, seven, four, three"), and I'd have to repeat them back to her. We got up to eighteen digits before I stumbled.

"I've never seen someone perform quite so well," she remarked.

She'd probably never tested a girl who had to memorize boys' phone numbers before her mother found them and threw them away.

That skill, combined with my financial need, helped me get into the Baldwin School. "Grace Kelly went there," my mother would tell anyone who would listen, as if I could be the next Grace Kelly.

• • •

With that statement, I started to hate Baldwin. My mother was working harder than ever to put food on the table, and these girls wouldn't eat? That's selfish, I thought, it's not a disease. You don't see poor people with anorexia, I reasoned. How were they going to tell me what black boys wanted? Just like my hip-hop songs said, they seemed to think their culture was the only one. My interaction with the white students and faculty soon became limited to pointing out how racist they were and how black I was. I was determined to stretch their "dare to question" motto until it snapped. I wanted out.

"How come you offer ten languages but they are all European languages?" I asked the school's headmistress.

"What do you want us to offer, Swahili?" she replied.

"Why not?" I responded. She looked at me, wrung her hands, and said she'd look into it.

The Berlin Wall came down and the school decorated the main hall with pictures celebrating its fall. The pictures were still there five months later when Nelson Mandela was freed from prison. No one in administration put up anything for him.

"How come you don't put up anything for Nelson Mandela?" I asked.

The next day, next to FREEDOM FOR EAST GERMANY! someone had stenciled in AND SOUTH AFRICA! I caught Miss Betty writing *Not really, just Nelson* next to the new addition.

When Christmas rolled around, I knew I had to figure out how to get myself kicked out of Baldwin. I believed my mother's and brother's mental health was on the line.

My brother had begged all fall for a collector's-edition GI Joe figurine, but because my mother had to save up to buy my school books and spring uniform, she couldn't afford any expensive toys. Under the tree was her GI Joe substitute, a big grab bag full of green plastic military men, the cheap ones that were frozen forever in war poses. My brother broke down sobbing. "You can't bend them at the waist like GI Joe!" he yelled.

"I thought these *were* GI Joes," my mother lied. There was no way she thought that a bag labeled AMERICAN HEROES! was the toy he wanted.

"I wanted the GI Joe Scuba Set!" my brother cried. "You can fill it with real water!" My mother went to the kitchen and came back with a bedpan she'd "borrowed" from her job to wash dishes in.

"You can fill this with real water," my mother said and then fell asleep under the tree. She had to go to work in a few hours.

"It's all your fault!" my brother whispered to me. "You and your stupid boyfriends and bad grades made Mom poor!"

He was right. I promised him I'd work harder to get kicked out, and if it didn't happen by next Christmas, I'd rob one of the rich white girls and buy him a GI Joe set myself.

I started the new year by writing up a list of demands for my school. *If you're so committed to diversity, we'd have rappers at our next music series,* I wrote, sure that asking for hip-hop would mean my expulsion.

How was I to know that my ceramics teacher's husband owned a recording studio? At the next music series, a struggling rapper and her backup dancers entertained the upper school. I waited to cause more disruption until I flirted with one of the dancers and secured him as my date to the tenth-grade dance. After the dance, I started up again. "I refuse to go to yet another anorexia and bulimia seminar because studies show black women don't have eating disorders," I told the headmistress. She agreed with me and I got a free period, while the other girls learned to love their bodies. "It makes me sick to my stomach that third-graders are allowed to call the cleaning women by their first names!" Soon after, there was a schoolwide memo that all faculty and staff were to be addressed as Mr. or Ms., unless they requested otherwise. "I want a full scholarship! I demand it as part of my reparations!" That I didn't get, but my mother didn't care. "All this work is worth it to get you a good education," she said, after pulling yet another double shift.

Damn, we're poor, I thought, the first time we pulled through the expansive wrought-iron gates of Baldwin. Our Chevy Nova was pulling up at the rear of a long row of Jaguars, Mercedeses, and Porsches. My new school was situated on twenty-three acres of lush greenery. The only brown patches seemed to be the baseball field, the janitorial staff, and me and my mother. It was the same neighborhood Will and I had gotten pulled over in.

"They're just regular people with a bit more money," my mother said, but I could tell she was overwhelmed, too. The school building itself looked like a castle. We got lost three times just trying to get to registration.

The highlight of my first day was learning that my Greek mythology teacher had a Mercedes Benz with a license plate that read TROY 1. I took a photo posing in front of her license plate to make my boyfriends jealous. ("Troy, who the fuck is Troy?") I hoped the jealousy would spur them into picking me up. In a car, the drive to school was forty-five minutes; to get there on public transportation, the journey stretched to two hours.

Like my grandmother's house before it, Baldwin had a whole new culture to learn. I was corrected when I referred to it as high school, it was *upper school*. There was no hallway; there were *corridors*. Who knew Mercedes made station wagons, and why would anyone buy a fly car like a Mercedes and mess it up by getting the station-wagon version? I'd gotten a job at Roy Rogers so I could pay for the expensive sneakers my mother refused to buy me; at Baldwin, new expensive sneakers were made fun of. These girls purposefully scuffed up their sneakers. It was almost as if they were embarrassed by their wealth. *Give it to me,* I thought.

My mom, despite her enthusiasm at having gotten me into Baldwin, had a bunch of things to learn as well. She always seemed blindsided by the things my scholarship didn't cover. Instead of issuing out-of-date science textbooks with titles like *It's Definite: The World Is Round* like public school did, we now had to buy a stack of new books every semester.

As soon as she recovered from the book sticker shock, I bought home a note detailing the school's mandatory after-school sports program. I had never played a team sport; "head, shoulders, knees, and toes" was the extent of my school physical activity.

"What's a cleat?" I asked my mother, reading the requirements for field hockey.

"Something else I have to pay for." She sighed. Neither of us knew what field hockey was, nor did the sales guy at our neighborhood sporting goods store. That's why he sold me a neon orange "Go Flyers!" street hockey stick. Wearing my Baldwin uniform on public transportation was bad enough without the added burden of being a black girl with a bright orange hockey stick.

"What school is that?" the girls from my neighborhood Catholic high school would sneer on the first bus I caught. When I transferred to the suburban rail line, the black domestics who caught the same train to clean houses would stare at me. On the train platform, I met other uniformed black students, all of us shuffling off to different schools but having the same tenseness with the domestics.

One girl who went to a school across the street from mine warned me about saying anything positive about my school in front of the younger housekeepers. "The older ones are fine; if they want to talk to you, it's only because they are proud of you," she said. She was right. My third week on the train, a group of older ladies asked me to sit near them. For the one-hour ride, they told me to "do them proud" and make sure I got good grades. "You don't want to end up cleaning their houses like we do," one said. What was I supposed to say, *Yeah, cleaning white folks' houses would suck?* I just smiled, looking over to make sure the younger domestics weren't about to jump me.

The day I had to take the hockey stick to school, I tried to hide it by dragging it behind me like an old blanket. A younger girl in a cleaning uniform tripped over it and yelled about how the "private school girls think they're smart but don't have any damn common sense." I felt like it was Christina and Tascha all over again.

Once I got onto the school grounds, life was gravy. Because I lived in the city, I was popular from the first day. Most of my Baldwin classmates viewed all parts of Philadelphia as dangerous. Not one had ever been there without her parents. I indulged their taste for spooky stories about the city, telling them about my subway fight and, when that became old news, I told them I'd seen someone get robbed (true, it was me; Christina stole my flute from my locker) and that I'd seen someone get shot (true, on TV). "That's just how it is in the city," I'd say, shaking my head like an old hardened cop.

I hoped that filling them up with firsthand accounts of incidents they'd never experienced would distract their attention from me and all the private school things I'd never experienced. Like, where the hell did they buy those wooden hockey sticks? When I saw everyone come to practice with the correct field-hockey stick, I again hid my orange one behind me. The two black students in my class noticed my discomfort.

"You should come to Black Student Union meetings," one said, eyeing my Day-Glo stick as if she'd seen this kind of mistake before. I made it to two BSU meetings. In the first, I listened as the seven students brought up grievances about the school. When they asked me how I liked it, I told them as long as no one was trying to beat me up, I was happy. Frowns all around. At the second meeting, I did my homework as they strategized about how to promote black culture around the school. A Frederick Douglass After-School Jam? Are they serious? I wondered. I decided to leave the BSU; I was the only black student who didn't go to the weekly meetings.

I'd have more time for blackness if it met my schedule, I thought. I lived farther from school than anyone else, and I hated having to give up the one night of the week I could actually make it home before 7 P.M. I secretly envied the white girls who were chauffeured home by their housewife mothers after hours of sweaty practice.

Still, it was nice being seen as *tough* and *urban,* two labels I didn't have a chance of obtaining with people who knew more about the Boonies. The only thing that stood between me and total school domination were the thirty pounds I had put on since puberty. In my neighborhood, the extra padding of layers I'd grown on my ass wasn't fat, it was *thickness,* a sign of womanhood. At school, I was constantly being given lessons by my classmates on how to lose weight.

Girls at Baldwin were catching anorexia like the flu. One girl stopped eating completely, and almost everyone else decided to join in. They'd have weight-loss clubs, where size-6 girls would extreme-diet down to a size 2. At lunch, girls would fill up their plates with food, so the faculty, who ate in the same lunchroom, wouldn't suspect anything. Instead of eating, these female leaders of tomorrow would shove the food around on their plates while asking mind-bending questions like "Would you rather have a fat face and a skinny body or a fat body and a skinny face?" Everyone wanted a fat body with a skinny face. They were pros at not eating, so they could lose body weight. "Face weight is there to stay," they all concurred.

I actually tried really hard not to eat, but the food was actually good there, for God's sake. The cafeteria ladies didn't just slap a half-warmed frozen chicken patty on your plate, they made sandwiches according to your instructions. "Don't be like them girls and not eat," the salad-bar tender told me. "I won't, Miss Betty," I said. For that, she reached around the grill and gave me extra fries. "I haven't had one of these students call me *Miss* yet," she said. "Your mother raised you right."

While everyone else got thinner, I gained more weight, thanks to Miss Betty's extra helpings. After three months, I gained a dress size.

"It's called *portions,* Angela," my mother said. "I love you whatever size you are, but my pocketbook doesn't. I can't afford new uniforms."

At lunch the girls cautioned me about my hips as I dug into cheese fries. "Black guys like meat on their woman's bones," I told the table.

"There isn't a boy in the world who wouldn't mind his girlfriend being a little skinnier," one girl said, and the table nodded in agreement.

With that statement, I started to hate Baldwin. My mother was working harder than ever to put food on the table, and these girls wouldn't eat? That's selfish, I thought, it's not a disease. You don't see poor people with anorexia, I reasoned. How were they going to tell me what black boys wanted? Just like my hip-hop songs said, they seemed to think their culture was the only one. My interaction with the white students and faculty soon became limited to pointing out how racist they were and how black I was. I was determined to stretch their "dare to question" motto until it snapped. I wanted out.

"How come you offer ten languages but they are all European languages?" I asked the school's headmistress.

"What do you want us to offer, Swahili?" she replied.

"Why not?" I responded. She looked at me, wrung her hands, and said she'd look into it.

The Berlin Wall came down and the school decorated the main hall with pictures celebrating its fall. The pictures were still there five months later when Nelson Mandela was freed from prison. No one in administration put up anything for him.

"How come you don't put up anything for Nelson Mandela?" I asked.

The next day, next to FREEDOM FOR EAST GERMANY! someone had stenciled in AND SOUTH AFRICA! I caught Miss Betty writing *Not really, just Nelson* next to the new addition.

When Christmas rolled around, I knew I had to figure out how to get myself kicked out of Baldwin. I believed my mother's and brother's mental health was on the line.

My brother had begged all fall for a collector's-edition GI Joe figurine, but because my mother had to save up to buy my school books and spring uniform, she couldn't afford any expensive toys. Under the tree was her GI Joe substitute, a big grab bag full of green plastic military men, the cheap ones that were frozen forever in war poses. My brother broke down sobbing. "You can't bend them at the waist like GI Joe!" he yelled.

"I thought these *were* GI Joes," my mother lied. There was no way she thought that a bag labeled AMERICAN HEROES! was the toy he wanted.

"I wanted the GI Joe Scuba Set!" my brother cried. "You can fill it with real water!" My mother went to the kitchen and came back with a bedpan she'd "borrowed" from her job to wash dishes in.

"You can fill this with real water," my mother said and then fell asleep under the tree. She had to go to work in a few hours.

"It's all your fault!" my brother whispered to me. "You and your stupid boyfriends and bad grades made Mom poor!"

He was right. I promised him I'd work harder to get kicked out, and if it didn't happen by next Christmas, I'd rob one of the rich white girls and buy him a GI Joe set myself.

I started the new year by writing up a list of demands for my school. *If you're so committed to diversity, we'd have rappers at our next music series,* I wrote, sure that asking for hip-hop would mean my expulsion.

How was I to know that my ceramics teacher's husband owned a recording studio? At the next music series, a struggling rapper and her backup dancers entertained the upper school. I waited to cause more disruption until I flirted with one of the dancers and secured him as my date to the tenth-grade dance. After the dance, I started up again. "I refuse to go to yet another anorexia and bulimia seminar because studies show black women don't have eating disorders," I told the headmistress. She agreed with me and I got a free period, while the other girls learned to love their bodies. "It makes me sick to my stomach that third-graders are allowed to call the cleaning women by their first names!" Soon after, there was a schoolwide memo that all faculty and staff were to be addressed as Mr. or Ms., unless they requested otherwise. "I want a full scholarship! I demand it as part of my reparations!" That I didn't get, but my mother didn't care. "All this work is worth it to get you a good education," she said, after pulling yet another double shift.

Finally, I knew the only way I would get to leave Baldwin was by convincing my mother I hated it. I caught her when she got her tuition bill for eleventh grade. "They lowered your scholarship!" she exclaimed. "People told me they do that the longer you're in the school. They know you don't want to leave once you get there, so they've got you hooked!"

"I don't have to go back," I said. "I hate it anyway. By the time I get home, I'm too tired. The white kids don't have to travel two hours!"

"Well, it's going to be like that all your life. You'll have to work twice as hard as white people to get to the same place," she said. "Look, I just don't think public school is right for you. There are too many distractions." I knew distractions meant *boys*.

"If I get into Girls' High, can I leave Baldwin?" I asked, grateful that Philadelphia had an all-girls public school. My mother looked again at the tuition bill and gave in.

"Only Girls' High. I don't want you around any boys," my mother said.

A few weeks later, I applied again to a series of public magnet schools, hoping my mother would change her mind about no boys if I got into one of the best schools. Girls' High was full, but I was accepted by the High School for Creative and Performing Arts, granted I passed a special "creative arts" test.

"I don't know about this. I said no boys," my mother said as we walked into the school. When the only boys she saw were a troop of dancers in full makeup demonstrating their ballet skills to prospective parents, she changed her mind. "Yes, this school will do."

I passed the entrance exam by writing about my orange hockey-stick incident and transferred to Creative and Performing Arts in the middle of eleventh grade. "If there is one behavior incident, you go back to the suburbs," my mother warned me. I made the honor roll on my first try and graduated with only one minor incident, which I never told my mother about. (I was punched in the face by a crackhead when Boyz II Men filmed their first music video outside our school. I was standing in the way while she was trying to steal a part of the set.) I graduated with a letter of acceptance from the University of Pennsylvania. Somehow, it didn't strike me as odd that I'd done all that work to escape one white private school and there I was going right back to another.

Nation of Islam Lite

In an unusual research project conducted in 1968, anthropologist Melville Herskovits measured the lightness of skin and width of facial features in Blacks of two different socioeconomic groups. . . . The well-to-do men were found to have generally lighter skin color, and their noses were an average of 3.8 millimeters narrower than those of men in the poorer segment of the research group. Similarily, the average lip thickness in the well-to-do group was 1 millimeter less than the thickness found in the other group.

—*Kathy Russell, Midge Wilson, and Ronald Hall,*
  The Color Complex: The Politics of Skin Color
  Among African Americans (*detailing the only kind of*
  study I wouldn't have signed up for in college,
  no matter how much it paid)

"You are so blessed. You got into one of the top schools in the country, and you can't go to church and thank God for that?" my mother said, shaking her head.

"I'm sorry, I have to work," I replied. I did have to work, because I had signed up to work every Sunday so I could get out of going to church. The Christian God was for white folks. So was that school I'd been accepted into and I had debated not even attending. My new boyfriend and I had plans to open up a nonprofit school for black children. After some thought, we decided that since so many black people worship the white man's educational degrees, my having a degree from an Ivy League school could help us convince more black parents to enroll their children.

Mah (short for Madani; he'd chosen the name for himself out of a book of Muslim baby names) was the love of my seventeen-year-old life. He was an intelligent hoodlum, the type of man we suddenly righteous black girls dream about. Mah had no problem punching someone in the face, but he also found time to go to museums with me and draw white people into debates on whether or not Egyptians were black ("Look in the artifacts case! That's a pick! Since when do white people use picks?"). The more white people he offended, the prouder I was.

Mah and I met on the subway. I was reading *The Autobiography of Malcolm X*. I wanted to read the book before Spike Lee's version hit theaters.

"It's so nice to see a sister dressed righteously and reading," Mah said, leaning over me. My outfit wasn't put together with righteousness in mind. I was a size 18, and the plus-size stores didn't stock too many skin-baring outfits. If I was a size 6, I'd have had half my ass hanging out.

My size didn't matter to Mah. During our first date, he told me that my mind was more important than my body. "White men want those skinny girls because they want to keep them small and controllable like children," Mah said. "I want a woman who can think for herself."

On our second date, we went to a black bookstore where he read to me from *How to Eat to Live* by Elijah Muhammad. I listened attentively and made plans to throw away all my mother's meat when I got home. We picked a new name for me from the same book he'd gotten his from. I left my given name at the bookstore register and left with Talibah—translation: *seeker of knowledge*.

"It's the perfect name for you," Mah said. "Even though you're light, your search for truth makes you blacker than most of the dark-skinned girls out here." Men, if you want to hook a biracial girl looking for acceptance from the black community, use that line. I was in bed with him the same night.

. . .

My mother hated Mah.

"I know that boy's mom didn't name him no Mahami Salami," she said, intentionally butchering his name. "I'm going to call him what his mother named him."

"Mom, please," I pleaded. She could at least respect the man I thought of as my husband-to-be, even if she insisted on still calling me by my slave name.

"Angela isn't a slave name. I gave you that name. And your last name isn't a slave name either. The Nissels came over here after slavery."

I had to admit she was right about the Nissel. Still, Talibah Nissel didn't sound very black, so I began to add an extra *l* to the end. Nis-*sell*, I'd tell people. "It's a Creole name."

By the time I started Penn, I was living pork-free and had cut the perm out of my hair. I was determined to be the blackest freshman there. I moved into the W.E.B. DuBois House, a dorm dedicated to the study of African American culture. Most white students seemed afraid of that dorm, so it was like I was going to a miniature black college inside a white school.

DuBois was one of Penn's many Living Learning Residence Halls. In addition to DuBois House, there was a modern language dorm for students who wanted to live like Parisians and a health residence for future doctors and nurses. DuBois, however, was the only residence hall that white students seemed to have issues with. Though it was open to people of all races, the campus newspaper often carried op-ed pieces about how divisive it was. White students often referred to it derisively as Da Boyz House.

Soon after I had unpacked my bags in DuBois, the campus newspaper ran a front-page photo of a homeless black man lying on the sidewalk with the caption *West Philadelphian*. I wrote a complaint letter to the editor. "My mother was raised in West Philadelphia! How insensitive, considering that the majority of the housekeeping staff who clean up vomit after your white frat-boy parties are West Philadelphians!" It wasn't published.

Soon after that photo, every corner of campus I went to, I'd hear white students complaining about being forced to go to school in West Philadelphia, "the scary ghetto." I'd hear this in front of the cafeteria workers who'd been working and living in the scary ghetto their whole lives. I overheard a girl on the Safety Van (the Penn van that transported students door to door so they wouldn't get robbed in the scary ghetto) telling a student how she'd just had a "spectacular interview" at Goldman Sachs in New York. "I hope I get it so I can move out of these slums." The van's driver, an older black man, shot an angry glance at her through the rearview mirror and then rubbed his hand over his entire face, as if he were adjusting his features to keep his composure. I had an image of my grandfather talking about his last job as a train porter. How he drove two hours to work and kept a tense smile on his face as white passengers looked down on him.

I decided to get off at the same stop as the Goldman Sachs interviewee did and gently scare the crap out of her. I followed her up the front stairs to her building, as if I lived in the same apartment complex. When her key was in the door, I tapped her on the shoulder. She gasped, as if prepared for me to rob her.

"All black people aren't trying to rob you, honey," I said, laughing. "I just heard you talking about your interview at Goldman Sachs. My father works in human resources there," I lied. "He grew up in West Philly—these slums, as you call them. I got your name off the van sign-in list, and I'm calling him first thing tomorrow." She reached for her rape whistle. I ran around the corner.

As freshman year rolled on, the already frequent derogatory newspaper columns about West Philadelphians and DuBois House seemed to increase tenfold. Instead of my dorm being a lively, happy safe haven for black students, it was as if someone had poured dust over it and painted it gray. Few people smiled when they walked through the doors. Students congregated around the front desk and complained about how much they hated Penn to Miss Lisa, the older receptionist, who looked after us like we were her children.

"Can you believe someone had the nerve to tell me I was only here because of affirmative action?" someone asked. "I got all A's in high school!"

"Why do we have to integrate with *them*? Why can't they walk their plates over to our table?" my roommate grumbled while she was brushing her hair. She'd just read the latest editorial accusing black students of being racist because they chose to eat together in the dining hall.

Finally, unable to limit their anger to complaints inside the safety of DuBois, a group of black students woke up at 5 A.M. and grabbed all the free school papers from every campus drop-off point and tossed them into a recycling bin. I watched as the students came back to the dorm refreshed, crying and laughing, finally releasing the hurt they felt after reading those articles every day. By evening, the incident had made national news.

To outsiders, it seemed as if every student in DuBois supported the mass disposal of the campus papers. In reality, it caused a small group of us to splinter off and separate ourselves from the paper tossers. Not because we thought throwing away free papers was stealing (as some news stations put it), but because we felt their efforts were too pacifist, too old-school-protest, too Negro-spiritual singing and hoping the white people would recognize the error of their actions and change.

"Mah, can you believe these backroads Negroes?" I said while we walked to a meeting of my new anti-paper-tosser group. Though Mah didn't attend Penn, he was welcomed. To turn away a brother because he didn't have higher education would have been too elitist for my activist friends.

I silently dubbed our group of eight Nation of Islam Lite, since one student, Terrell, who used to be in the Nation of Islam, would bring VCR tapes of ministers' lectures. We'd watch them on Friday nights while the majority of DuBois students were out partying at the only black frat house on campus.

"They are so *Negro* to be out drinking." Terrell sighed. "Don't they know that one day a white man is going to realize that all the black students are in one place and tear-gas the house?"

"That's the quickest way to kill black people: Invite them to a party and then drop a missile on the house," Mah concurred, pressing PLAY on the VCR.

"Ooh, 'The Goddamn White Man'!" a sister in a head wrap cooed. "That's my favorite tape!"

"The Goddamn White Man" was a lecture given by a minister about all the destruction caused by—well, the goddamn white man. It made sense to me. White people were always trying to blame black people for violence, when in reality they were the ones doing all the dirt. God knows I had been reading about their wars and their enslavement of brown people forever. Every nation they touched was left ravaged. Even my ex-boyfriend, who got caught stealing cars, was doing it on commission from white-owned auto body shops for parts.

"Yeah! How come when *they* riot, it's called a party?" a girl about my complexion screamed as the tape played. "The Boston Tea Party wasn't a party! That was a damn looting riot!"

"Show me one good white person," the minister on the tape implored. I couldn't think of one. Not my relatives, not my non-child-support-paying dad, and certainly no one so far at the University of Pennsylvania.

Sometimes, we'd have speakers at our group. I was floored by a white guy who believed that white people were prone to violence because they were from colder climates. "White people are from climates where nothing grows. After thousands of years of fighting, only the strongest, most violent whites have survived," he explained. He even suggested that white people were the missing link that anthropologists had been searching for. "They call black people monkeys and chimps, but have you ever seen the skin of a chimp? It's white! Their hair is straight, just like white people's!" I was so excited after that speaker. "If a white person is saying that about his own people, it has to be true," I said, not realizing that—by that reasoning—if a middle-class person in the Boonies said poor blacks were just niggas, that had to be true, too.

My love for the white speaker was my first major argument within the group. Malik, whose father was in the Black Panther

Party and had discovered wiretaps in the organization's phone, told me it was a sign I still had a slave mentality if I believed some- one just because he was white. He was right. Why was it easier to believe something because a white guy said it? We'd been hearing tape after tape of black people saying basically the same thing about white people. I apologized.

We learned about CoIntelPro, the Tuskeegee experiment, and hormones in meat. I became paranoid and cautious, though more so in front of group members than in private. I proclaimed myself a vegan but would sneak off and eat Twix bars by the case, even though they were on the "banned food list" because they had gelatin in them. ("That's a pork-based product, queen," Terrell said.)

I'd bend the rules more blatantly when it came to money. The rule of "Trust no white person, especially those in medicine and government," isn't an easy task if you're broke. Anytime a campus- sponsored medical study came up that paid more than twenty-five dollars, I'd be the first one on the sign-up sheet. I eased my guilty conscience by never giving answers I judged would make the black race look bad. On a survey of campus sexual activity, I checked VIRGIN. When asked how many hours a day I spent studying, I filled in the SIX HOURS OR MORE bubble, the maximum time.

One day I checked the psychology board and found a study that specifically wanted freshmen and was paying four hundred dollars. I could buy a lot of leather Africa pendants and meatless burgers with that, I thought.

There was a pretest to see who qualified for the study. I couldn't figure out what types of people they were looking for from the tone of the questions, so I just answered truthfully.

How was my adjustment to college life coming? I checked off D: NOT SO WELL.

How had I been feeling the past couple weeks? D: NOT SO WELL.

A week later, there was a message on my voice mail from the Psychology Department. They wanted me to come in right away. I got excited and started spending the four hundred dollars in my head, I'd never had that much money at one time. I wondered if I'd get cash or a check. If it was a check, I'd take it to the bank and ask for one hundred-dollar bill and three hundred ones, so the wad would look really thick. I'd save half and spend half. Forget the Africa pendants, I'd get Mah some of that herb Goldenseal he needed to flush the marijuana out of his system before he applied for a job with the Philadelphia Gas Department; then *he* could buy *me* pendants.

When I got to the Psychology Department, the receptionist directed me back to a closet-size teaching assistant's office where three twenty-something white men sat. I recognized only one from the day I took the pretest. They said hello warmly; all six eyes watched me as I took the only open seat.

"Ms. Nissel, we finished scoring your test and you don't qualify for the study," said the one in the middle. I wondered why they couldn't have just told me that over the phone. I broke a sweat to come over here, I thought.

"Based on your test answers, we feel you should talk to someone. You seem to show signs of depression," he continued.

The room felt smaller and stuffier than it already was. I felt trapped and angry. I was about to cry. How dare white guys who knew nothing about me other than one hundred answers in a number-2 pencil tell me I needed help? Was this part of the psychology experiment? Let's see what happens when three grown white guys lock a black girl in a room and tell her she's crazy during her first semester of classes?

While I was trying to figure out what to do, who to curse out, they offered to give me the names of some psychiatrists.

I got up and choked back tears. "I come in here to help you with your study and you tell me I'm crazy?"

"Well, we don't like to use the word *crazy*," I heard a voice say before I ran down the hallway.

I powered back to DuBois with my head down. If anyone said anything to me I was liable to explode into tears. I'd been doing that a lot lately for no apparent reason. I'd get an A on a test and I'd cry. Hormones, I reasoned. I was living with three women and our periods were all shifting toward one another.

Terrell was in the library. I pulled him into the hall and told him what had just happened.

"It was probably a government program designed to get information on black college students," he said, rubbing my shoulders. He told me not to worry about the depressed part. "Black women are too resilient to get depressed," he said. "You don't ever hear about women in Africa taking Prozac," he added.

Yes, of course. A depressed black woman was about as unthinkable as a feminist black woman. Righteous black people knew the two didn't go together. My mood swings were definitely hormonal. I went to my room, where I felt relieved for about ten minutes, and then started crying again. I called Mah, who echoed Terrell's thoughts.

"Don't let them white boys get in your head. They just want to drug you," he said. "Do you think our ancestors had the luxury of depression when they were being whipped and working in those fields?" Again, I felt better for ten minutes, and then for no apparent reason I started crying again.

I needed a woman's perspective. I started walking over to Milani's room. Milani was my best friend on campus. She was also biracial and had attended a few Nation of Islam Lite meetings earlier in the year. She'd stopped going because she was in love and her new boyfriend, Tamas, needed her to braid his hair every Sunday. He was a Hebrew Israelite, and according to the rules of his religion it was a sin to cut your hair.

Milani and I looked so much alike people thought we were twins despite the fact that she was two years ahead of me. Occasionally, people would ask us how we could hate white people when we ourselves were half white.

"Half white doesn't make you all white," she'd say. "One drop of black blood makes you black," I'd chime in—using the words I'd first heard from my mother but now heard all the time.

Milani and I both thought we looked a little better and a little

blacker with a tan. We'd sneak off after meetings to get a dose of
UV radiation from Sun on the Run tanning salon. We'd make self-
deprecating jokes to the staff at the tanning salon, sure that they'd
never had black customers before; then we'd go study together
and talk about the goddamn white man.

I had a suspicion that her boyfriend, Tamas, didn't like me. Milani would tense up when we were together. The first time we met,
he questioned me excessively about my background, particularly
my father. What country were his ancestors from? Was *his* father
from Italy? I figured he was just another paranoid black national-
ist, so I had answered his every question in detail.

When I got to Milani's room, Tamas opened the door. He
greeted me halfheartedly and stomped out. I noticed that she had
redecorated in the past few days; her Africa poster had been replaced with a gold-tone Star of David ornament.

Milani looked like she had been crying. I thought she was
about to tell me that someone had died. I felt embarrassed for interrupting her with my trivial problem.

"Girl, I was just upset at something these white boys did to me
today," I said, waving my hand as I said the words, trying to indi-
cate that it wasn't a big deal. Milani pressed me for what had happened.

I told her, laughing at how silly it all was.

"Talibah, they're telling the truth. *You* could be depressed." She
emphasized the word *you* as if to say, *You could but not me.*

She went on. "I know this is going to come as a shock to you,
but we can't be friends anymore. Tamas has taught me the truth
about race: A child is the race of his father," she said. "You're an
Edomite. I am from the tribe of Judah, God's chosen tribe," she
added.

I looked at her like she was insane. Was she saying what I
thought she was—that although we both had a white parent, she
was more black?

"Are you sure your father isn't Sicilian?" she asked, with hope
in her voice. "Sicilians are from the Tribe of Judah. You know, the
whole Moor thing and all."

I almost lied and said he was. Unfortunately, only his mother was Sicilian and women's genes didn't seem to count in her new faith. I walked out of her room and slammed the door. I was upset at losing a friend, but more upset that another group had decided I still wasn't black enough. *After all the work I'd put in, not eating meat and missing parties?* At least I still have Mah, I thought.

Two days after Milani broke the news to me that I was the same white devil I'd been railing against, Mah accused me of giving him syphilis.

"Are you sure you didn't cheat on me? Then how come I'm on the white man's antibiotics?" he asked, shaking the orange pill bottle in my face. For a week, I scared myself sick, thinking perhaps I had had dormant syphilis for years and had given it to my black prince. Only after I came up negative for syphilis twice did he admit that when he wasn't spreading the news about the evils of the white man, he enjoyed going to parties and having unprotected sex with women in bathrooms. He also admitted that he had another girlfriend on the side who would be more fit to run his school. As if the week wasn't bad enough with losing a friend and finding out I was going to Edomite Hell, he pulled out her photo. She was that perfect brown toast color I'd been trying to achieve by all my hours at Sun on the Run. She also had on short shorts. A far cry from the conservatively dressed African queen he claimed to prefer.

That was the straw that broke the depressed black woman's back. That night, I slept for twenty hours but was still unable to get out of bed. When I finally rolled over, I used all my strength to turn to PSYCHIATRISTS in the phone book.

"I think I need to see someone," I whispered into the phone, so that my strong black female roommates couldn't hear me.

I never made it to the psychiatrist that year. I didn't make it anywhere outside of my dorm room, actually. I spent all my energy faking normalcy in my voice when people called to see why I wasn't in class. I told some people I had the flu, some people I had asthma, some people that I was just really busy with schoolwork. I wished everyone would leave me alone but secretly hoped that someone could tell I was lying and come rescue me. I wanted to die, but the wish made me mad at myself. I didn't have the energy to commit suicide, and I was mad at myself for that, too. I took incompletes in all my classes.

Sophomore year, I moved off campus. Living alone was the perfect incubator for depression. There were no roommates to notice that I hadn't taken a shower or that I'd been crying all day. I could wake up, order in Ben and Jerry's, and cry myself back to sleep. Finally, when I received potential failure notices from all my classes, I decided to hit the Yellow Pages again.

Though it would have been easier, there was no way I was going to the university's Student Health Center, even though rumor had it they were dispensing Prozac as freely as they did condoms. I was not going to risk someone seeing me in the psychiatric waiting room. I looked through the phone book until I found a doctor with an ethnic-sounding last name.

Dr. Nami talked to me for about ten minutes and gave me a pocket-size trial pack of Prozac. She said it might take some time to feel better, but I felt slightly better just having the drugs in my pocket. The receptionist at Dr. Nami's office informed me that, to get additional visits, I'd have to call my insurance and get approved. I'd never had to do that for a doctor's visit before.

"Only for mental health visits and chiropractors, the stepchildren of medicine," she said.

Talking to a phone customer-service rep is a challenge for me even on a *non*depressed day. While most people get frustrated pushing touch-tone buttons and talking to a computerized voice, I get mad when I key in the wrong combination of numbers and actually have to talk to a human representative. I prefer computers. Computers don't come in with an attitude after being stuck in traffic. They don't decide they hate your voice and put you on hold forever. Computers are one of the few places where everyone has a level playing field. You get out what you put in, without prejudice.

I punched every button on my touch-tone phone, attempting not to get transferred to a human being. Every time I heard "Please hold for the next available representative," I'd hang up. After two hours of that game, I gave in. I was transferred to a male customer-service rep who sounded about seventeen years old and had only half of his attention on me. I heard the rustle of fast-food wrappers in the background. The customer-service rep's voice was robotic and his words were separated with long pauses, like he was reading a script from a slow-moving computer.

"Hello"—long pause, sound of him repeatedly hitting the space bar—"my name is Tad. What can I help you with"—pause, sound of him typing—"this afternoon?"

I told Tad I had to get approval to see a psychiatrist. I imagined he would transfer me to a doctor or fax some forms to my nearest Kinko's so I could pick them up.

"Sure, I can help you with that, I just have to"—thirty-second pause—"ask you some safety questions."

What the hell are safety questions? Like, do I know what a solid double line on a highway means?

"Sure," I replied, hesitantly.

"How many times have you seen a psychiatrist in the past year?"

This was too embarrassing. I had barely got up the nerve to talk to a psychiatrist and now I was letting a teenager—who was probably reading *Maxim* magazine as he talked to me—know how crazy I felt.

I held my finger to the phone's receiver, ready to hang up. *How many times have you seen a psychiatrist?* is not a safety question, I thought. Whose safety is that question for, the financial safety of the insurance company? Why don't they just call it what it is, a question about my past psychological state? Why the dumbed-down talk? I hate this. I hate everyone.

I took a deep breath. "I've been to a psychiatrist once, but I can't go again until I get approval from you."

I felt like Tad was typing *Failure* into my file, but I held in there, answering *no* when he asked me if I heard voices or had thoughts of harming people. I said *yes* when he asked if I had interrupted sleeping patterns. I wanted to ask him some questions about himself, since he had my whole life on the screen in front of him, like what brand of chips was he chewing in my ear? I restrained myself from doing that.

"Do you have thoughts of suicide?"

"Yes."

"Right now?"

"Yes. Because of how long this phone call is taking," I said. There was a long pause before he asked his next question.

"Okay, we're almost done. Can you verify your current address for me?"

I did. I could hear what sounded like him pounding on his keyboard.

"My computer is going slow; please hold for a second," he said.

While I was holding, there was a knock on my door. I looked through the peephole. *Cops. Oh, my goodness.* I opened the door.

Before me stood two police officers: Officer Grey, a beefy bulldog-looking middle-aged white guy with the kind of long mustache that must be fun to twirl in the mirror when no one is watching, and his partner, Officer Jenkins. She was a younger black female cop with a stylish haircut partially tucked under her cap. She looked like someone I might enjoy clubbing with if I wasn't so depressed.

"Are you Angela Nissel?" Officer Grey asked me. I nodded.

"Do you want to kill yourself?"

I couldn't believe it. Tad had called the cops on me.

"No! I don't want to kill myself!"

Officer Grey tilted his head and looked at my neck.

"Then what's that mark on your neck?"

"I burned myself with a curling iron!" I said. After I found out Mah was cheating, I gave up on natural no-fuss hairstyles. I was through with attracting righteous men for a while.

I looked to the black officer for help. Surely, she with her perm would back me up. "Won't you tell him it's a curling-iron burn?" I pleaded.

"Well, it does *look* like a curling iron burn," she said. I laughed out loud at the seriousness of their faces and the thought of a suicidal girl crying out, "I can't straighten my hair or my life out!" and holding a hot iron up to her neck.

It was the first time I'd laughed in over two weeks. Unfortunately, cops don't like it when you laugh at them.

"We have to take you to the hospital," Officer Grey said, while Officer Jenkins radioed something into her walkie-talkie about having a "Four-oh-four."

I asked them for permission to grab a few things and they kept a close eye on me while I did it. While I'm sure word was spreading through my building that cops were at my door, two EMTs showed up. The male EMT looked like he could be a cover model for *Black Bodybuilders*.

Why, when I was being taken to a mental hospital, did the sexiest EMT ever have to show up?

"Ma'am, I have to strap you to this gurney," the sexy EMT said.

"Are you serious? I'm not crippled! This is so embarrassing!" I screamed.

"It's for insurance reasons," he answered dryly, like I was wasting his time. I supposed crazy pickups are less exciting than heart attacks.

I hopped up on the gurney, not wanting to annoy the sexy EMT. He offered some advice to me as he started rolling me down the hallway. "If you cough a lot, your neighbors will think you're *really* sick instead of being taken away for something mental."

He was right. What would all my black neighbors think if I was wheeled away without any apparent signs of distress? As we pushed farther down the hallway, I started coughing slowly. By the time we left my apartment building, I was hacking like my whole life was caught in my throat.

Crazy Spa Interlude

Welcome to the Crazy Spa

We know you have a lot on your mind and hope you'll find this guide useful in answering your general questions about what to expect here. If you have more specialized questions, like "When will my brain neurons stop misfiring?" please ask your doctor.

In your first few days, just try to relax and enjoy your all-inclusive stay. If you find it hard to relax, we'll give you something to help you— probably something injectable.

Check-In

There is no set check-in time. We'll accept you through our Emergency Room whenever your doctor or the police decide your major depression, schizophrenia, bipolar disorder, anxiety disorder, or postpartum psychosis is threatening your safety or the safety of others around you.

Intake

An orderly will escort you from the E.R. to the Psychiatric Unit. When you and the orderly arrive at the psychiatric floor, you'll think that there is not much difference between that floor and the "normal" patient floors. Then you'll notice that you and the orderly must be buzzed in to the psych unit through steel-framed bulletproof-glass double doors. Those doors are there for your safety.

After being buzzed in, the orderly will deposit you in front of the nurses' station, and a nurse will give you a pencil and a test. For your safety, the pencil is barely sharpened. The test is called the MMPI (Minnesota Multiphasic Personality Inventory) and has over 500 questions. You'll be thinking, Why couldn't I have filled out this test during the eight hours I had in the damned Seclusion Room? Don't get upset. This is for you. Everything here is for you. The MMPI will help the doctors clarify your diagnosis.

Other mental health patients will be sitting in front of the nurses' station while you take the test. Some will be reading, some will be sleeping, some will be bitching about their meds. For the most part, they'll all look pretty normal, like your next-door neighbor or your teacher's aide. Actually, that *may be* your teacher's aide. Don't be embarrassed that she sees you're in the mental ward. As long as she has on a pa-tient's ID bracelet, she's in here, too.

Don't be afraid that one of the patients will go crazy at any moment. They're all wondering the same thing about you because you're a new admit and have yet to take any medication. One of the patients may attempt to break the ice and ask, "Is this your first time?" You can answer or not an-swer. Everyone here understands you're having a bad day.

Frisking / Confiscation

During intake the nurse may say to you, slowly and loudly as if she is speaking to a kindergartener, "Now, you don't have anything hidden in your pockets that you can cut with, do you?" Don't get upset. Some people, even hospital staff, confuse mental illness with complete f-ing mental retardation.

After you finish the test, all you'll want to do is lie down so people stop staring at you, but first you will be frisked for sharps and anything that you could use to set yourself or other patients on fire. Things that will be confiscated include but are not limited to:

- Plastic knives
- The shoelaces from your shoes
- Belts and pants drawstrings
- Anything with glass (framed photos, mirrors, etc.)
- Wire from your spiral notebooks
- Dental floss
- Balloons, plastic bags, and condoms
- Curling irons and hot combs

You will get everything back when you check out or when your doctor deems you sane enough to use them. Don't think anyone is singling you out—look around. Even the senior citizens' pants are hanging somewhere between their upper thighs and their knees because we took their belts. They look like old people in young, saggy, gangsta-rapper clothing. Once you emerge from your depression and can laugh at things, you'll see that this is actually a comical sight.

After your frisking/confiscation session, Hospital Administrative Staff will come around and talk to you about advance directives and living wills. I know it's a shame to taunt you with so many things related to death if you're in for a failed suicide, but we promise that you'll feel better in a few weeks.

Oceanfront Views

If you find yourself getting seasick, look around: Almost everything on our ward has been painted blue or green. These are calming, tranquil colors; we want you to relax and let us take care of your brain. There is no red or yellow here; those stimulating colors can cause agitation and hunger (think of one fast-food restaurant that doesn't have one of those colors in their logo). We wouldn't want to agitate you *and* make you hungry, because around here you don't get too much to eat. Whatever you do eat, you have to be able to cut with a spork because plastic knives are too sharp (see under Frisking).

Our entire unit is designed to reduce the amount of sensory stimulation you have, but if you do see any reds or yellows and they make you feel angry or unsafe, see a nurse.

Your Living Quarters

Note: If you're a celebrity, you will not have a room on the psychiatric unit. You will be given a room on one of the physical illness floors, so no one will suspect that you have problems with your brain. For more information, see Jane Pauley's memoir, page 321, or ask your doctor for our brochure entitled "Special Treatment."

For regular blue- and white-collar folks, our ward is equipped with thirty single-occupancy patient rooms. That's right! Unlike cancer and stage-three AIDS patients, you don't have to share your room with anyone! Other patients are not allowed in your room. There is a speaker above your bed. Periodically, you will hear voices through that speaker, including the nurse's aide who wakes you up at 7 A.M. and the one who announces that lunch is now being served. If you're alone in your room and you hear voices other than the one coming from your speaker, see a nurse.

Visitors

Don't worry if no one in your family will come see you because you're in a mental hospital. Soon after your 7 A.M. wake-up, you'll have about seven visitors: your main attending doctor and a group of terrified-looking medical residents who stare at you from the foot of your bed. You will see the thought bubbles forming over their heads: WHEN WILL MY GODDAMNED PSYCH ROTATION BE OVER? Besides this fun bunch, any family and friends who haven't written you off can visit between the hours of 5 P.M. and 9 P.M.

Level Numbers

Remember on the first day of school when your teacher would say, "Everyone starts with an A"? Here on the mental ward, everyone starts with a zero. When you first enter the unit, you are assigned a privilege level that starts at Level 0 (a staff member checks on you every five minutes to make sure you have not killed yourself, and you are not allowed off the locked unit for any reason). The highest level is 5, which means you can travel unaccompanied outside the hospital for up to four hours. The dry-erase board on the wall by the nurses' station will list your privilege level next to your name, in addition to the name of your attending doctor.

Being a Level 0 isn't easy. It can be downright frustrating at times. As a Level 0, you will not have a phone in your room because cords are dangerous. Because you can't talk on the phone, you might feel frustrated and caged in, so you may wish to venture into the hall to let out steam by playing pool or Ping-Pong. Unfortunately, there will be no balls, pool sticks, or paddles on either table, so you can't play. You have to earn your way toward using them again—you are a zero.

As you become more sane, you will be granted more privileges. At Level 1 you may use the phone at the nurses' station for quick five-minute calls, and they'll only check on you every half hour. When you move up to a Level 2, you may use balls, sticks, and paddles. At Level 3 you may use a blow dryer and curling iron on your hair and go on afternoon and evening nurse-facilitated smoke breaks. During these outdoor smoke breaks, you will walk along the side of the hospital in your open-back gown with your smoking-patient friends and pray no one you know sees you. A Level 4 means you may leave the unit for an hour at a time unaccompanied as long as your doctor writes you an authorization to leave on pass (LOP). Level 5, the "I'm almost free" level, means you can walk around wherever you want for four hours.

No matter what your level, a nurse will come around every half hour at night with a flashlight to make sure you're okay. When you see the flashlight in your room, please raise your hand if you're awake. If you don't see the light, see a nurse.

Medications

Everyone receives medications at the same time. When you hear the speaker voice announce "medication time," report to the nurses' station. Some patients will stare at you when you are given your pills. Don't worry, there is nothing on your face; they are looking at your meds. If you are being given a strong psychotropic or painkiller, some patients may ask you what you told the doctor to get that "good stuff." Don't tell them. Don't even think of trying to trade your pills. The nurse will check under your tongue to make sure you have swallowed them.

Group Activities

Another way to earn a higher privilege level is to participate fully in group activities; they are the heart and soul of your stay. Socialization via group activities is important to get you ready to go back to the biggest group of all: the outside world. For this reason, at Crazy Spa your meals are your first group activity. You will have all meals in the cafeteria across from the nurses' station.

Another group is Medication Education Therapy, where you sit in a circle with a nurse-practitioner and discuss your drugs and their side effects with other patients. It can be scary, wondering if it's worth it to trade your mental disorder for "brain shivers, loss of libido, and recurrent cystic acne," but in the group you'll also trade sex and makeup tips to help you deal with the horrible side effects. (Don't borrow anyone's lingerie; it's unsanitary.)

> *"Fuck you! I'm the son of God and I don't need any of your damned medication!"*
> —Jeff Smith, Level 0
>
> *"I love this place."*
> —Homeless guy
>
> *"I'm going to run away on my next smoke break."*
> —Lisa Lee, Level 4

Another exciting group you'll not want to miss is Occupational Therapy. Occupational Therapy sounds like someone will be helping you find a job, but that's not at all what it's about. (Actually, if you have a job, keep your mouth shut about your mental illness when you go back to it so your boss won't try to find ways to fire you.)

Occupational Therapy is a sort of arts and crafts. You cut out photos from magazines and make collages to describe your emotions. If you're not allowed scissors yet (Level 2), you have to rip the magazine photos out with your hands. How you went from being CFO of a Fortune 500 company to ripping up magazines with your hands like a savage may frustrate you. You know this collage won't help deal with your overflowing in-box when you get back to your office, but just go with it; that's the only way you'll ever leave Crazy Spa. If you feel you can't deal with it, see a nurse.

Thank you for choosing (being forced to choose) Crazy Spa. Remember: This is your time. Our primary focus is you, as long as your insurance doesn't run out. If it does, we'll let you know. And we'll probably ask for this pamphlet back.

You Can't Do a Drive-by
from a Wheelchair

A new study that involved surveying 90,000 adolescent U.S. students showed that those who considered themselves to be of mixed race were more likely than others to suffer from depression, substance abuse, sleep problems, and various aches and pains.

—*UNC News Services, October 10, 2003*

I spent eight hours in the Emergency Room or, to be more specific, eight hours in the Seclusion Room, which is the ER's "safe" room, which means it's free of anything a mentally ill person could use as a weapon. It's painted bright white and furnished with only a mattress and a sheet that smells faintly of bleach. The sheet is so thin it's see-through, so you couldn't possibly smother yourself with it, and if you tried to hang yourself it would just collapse into a pile of white dust under the strain of your body weight.

Eight hours in that all-white room gave me a lot of time to think. Mostly I thought about being black and crazy, how I'd let the whole race down by losing my mind. Maybe I should just hand in my Black Pass now and go back to being mixed.

When my mother, my brother, and I lived with my grandmother, she didn't allow any woman younger than herself to complain about anything. Getting down and depressed was just something black women had to deal with, something to push through, not something to roll over and let crush you. Right before she ate dinner, my nana would say, "I'm sick and tired of being sick and tired," like a sort of grace. I thought she invented the saying until I was grown and went to the African American History Museum and learned it was Fannie Lou Hamer, a black civil rights activist, who first spoke those words. When Hamer was jailed following a nonviolent protest, white cops forced black prisoners to pummel her with a blackjack. Even then she didn't get depressed: just "sick and tired."

My grandmother's predinner sighs, coupled with the understanding nods and umm-hmms of her church friends, seemed to be her antidepressant. With that and her Personal Lord and Savior on Sundays, she'd be just fine, thank you. In her house, the popular phrase "Black don't crack" meant black women didn't get wrinkles and they didn't have nervous breakdowns.

Of course, if my grandmother didn't allow grown women to complain, we little kids couldn't do it either. If my brother and I even sang a stanza of "It's the Hard Knock Life" we would be sat down and forced to listen to an audio tour of the white homes she cleaned when she was our age. "Aren't you glad you don't have to scrub white women's floors?" "Yes, Nana," we knew to reply in unison.

How could I get so low? I'd never had to scrub a white chick's floor. I was attending a posh Ivy League school with rich white girls who grew up having their floors cleaned, and still somehow my body and mind had given up on me. Congratulations, Angela. This is what your mom marched on Washington for: so you could vote and have a mental breakdown right with the white crazy people. Let freedom ring!

Oh, my God, my mother. What if she gets nervous when she calls my apartment and I don't answer? I knew her, she'd start calling hospitals. There was no way I was going to let my mother find out I was hospitalized. No sense both of us being disappointed in me. I rang the bell for the nurse.

"Did the cops tell you my name? I can't have my mother knowing I'm in here," I explained when the nurse rushed in. "What can I do?" I pleaded. I thought the nurse would be annoyed with my request and would reply with "What can you do? You can try being sane," but she nodded knowingly and took my ID bracelet off. A few minutes later, she came back with a reprinted one. My new name was Jane Doe.

Maybe I shouldn't be hiding from my mother, I thought. Maybe she has information about my father's side of the family that will help my diagnosis. That has to be where this weakness originated. Maybe Milani's new religion is right: It's my weak white genes that have me doomed. I wonder if I can go to her Hebrew Israelite meeting with a bottle of Prozac and a PowerPoint presentation detailing the mental inferiority of mulattoes with a white father. Would they accept me like I accepted the white man who said all white people are evil because their ancestors lived in the snow?

The weird part about being depressed (at least for me) was that a tiny part of my brain was still seeing things as I used to see things predepression. When I was with Mah, even if I didn't question all the race rules out loud, I always questioned them internally. When he told me that the saying *A dog is man's best friend* meant that white men liked to sleep with dogs, I thought, That's the dumbest thing I ever heard. I grew up with a white man, and he didn't fondle our dogs!

"Black women should always cover three-fourths of their body," he'd admonish me, adding that this kept us from unwanted male attention: namely, rape.

Why don't men learn to control their dicks? I'd think.

With depression, my internal questioning voice morphed from a sarcastic shout to a scared muffled whisper. Perhaps, maybe, could it be that depression has nothing to do with race? Maybe? the small sane part in my brain asked.

With 99 percent of my brain screaming that, no, it was all me and my weaknesses that caused me to be in an emergency room with a panic button, it was really hard to hear one lone dissenter.

After a spell of fighting to pay more attention to that tiny internal voice, I started tuning it out because it became more of a torturous tease. *Psssst. . . . This is what a normal brain used to feel like, and you're never getting back there.*

Thankfully, both the small sane part of me and the depressed part wanted to go to sleep (thin mattress and bleachy sheet be damned; I was bored), so I closed my eyes. I dreamed I had completed college and was at an all-white resort spa getting weight-loss treatments.

Lord, get me through this so I can know if a seaweed wrap really does help you lose inches, I thought, when I woke up. Maybe that's it. Maybe I just need to lose weight to be happier. No, I thought. Only white girls care about weight.

Tuesday, 6 P.M. Pt slept. Burn on neck.
An orderly came to roll me up to the Psychiatry Unit.

"Insurance reasons?" I asked, getting strapped onto the gurney.

"No, it's so you won't try to run away before we get upstairs," he said.

At first, I laughed. I had on foam slippers with no grip on the bottom; how was I going to run anywhere? As we rolled through the halls, I got nervous. Did the orderly think I would run because I'm crazy or because the psychiatric unit is full of freaks? Would I see the homeless guy from the subway who thought nothing of breaking into casual masturbation? I imagined some crazy chick who wanted to feel all over my face like blind people do in movies when they fall in love with a sighted person. By the time the orderly pressed the button to have us buzzed through the locked doors, I had convinced myself that I was going to have to fight all the other patients one by one. I fixed my face to look as rough as my insides felt.

When I was wheeled to the nurses' station, my face relaxed. If I had to fight, I would easily win. Sitting on the couches around the nurses' station was a bunch of frail-looking old white ladies, two of them so old their skin was see-through. The old white women gave me a quick nonjudgmental once-over.

"Shit, I thought you were Food Services. I'm hungry," one said, and went back to watching television.

A nurse walked over to me.

"Welcome," she said. I stared at her.

She approached one of the old ladies and asked if she could make room on the couch for me.

"Rose, just scoot over a bit so our new patient can take her MMPI test," the nurse said.

"I want to go home! You will not touch me!" Rose snapped. The women looking at the television laughed.

"Rose, please slide over and make room," the nurse said again.

"I want to go home! You will not touch me! I want to go home!" Rose repeated, digging her nails into the couch cushions.

Rose wasn't budging from her seat; I had to respect that. I have a thing in my heart for crotchety old ladies, the ones who know they are going to pass away any day now so they talk to anyone anyway they damn well please. I would find out later that Rose was suffering from combination Alzheimer's and dementia, and "You will not touch me! I want to go home!" is pretty much all she said.

"I can take the test here," I volunteered from my wheelchair. The nurse handed me the MMPI and I started filling out the 500-plus questions, using my lap as a desk.

True-or-false question number 41 of the MMPI: "At times I think I am no good at all." This question seemed just a slight variation of MMPI true-or-false question number 35: "I certainly feel useless at times." Hmmm. Were they trying to confuse me? Is this a trick question? What would a real crazy person answer so I can be sure to answer the opposite way? What answers did I put on the Penn psych test that got me here in the first place?

A Food Services worker buzzed through the bulletproof doors, pushing a metal cart stacked with food trays. The old women rose from their seats, searched through the trays, and then sat down together in the cafeteria and began eating in silence.

Soon after, while I was answering *False* to question number 87, "I was suspended from school one or more times for bad behavior," an announcement crackled through a loudspeaker above my head. *Dinner has arrived in the cafeteria.*

As soon as that announcement was made, a rainbow coalition of crazy people came around the corner and descended on the tray cart. Soon there were about twenty-five people eating dinner and, out of that number, ten were black. To be exact, there were eight black females and two black males. *Damn, about the same skewed percentage as my dorm. All the good black men must really be gay or in prison.*

Just as soon as I got a little happy that I wasn't the only crazy black in the world, I decided to withdraw that emotion. I didn't want to be down with crazy people, no matter what race they were. I can't accept being labeled crazy for the rest of my life. It's going to be harder for me to get life insurance and health insurance, and antidepressants are very expensive.

Most of the patients had finished their dinner when I was still working on my last set of MMPI questions. I was tired, and I really wanted to start a random selection of true and false answers without reading the corresponding questions, but I figured that, with my luck, my random answers would score out to NO HOPE FOR RE-HABILITATION and they'd ship me off to a lab where I would share space with a monkey and pray for PETA to rescue me.

I was almost on my last question when a young woman who appeared to be around my age sat across from my wheelchair. She had flawless cocoa skin, her face was perfectly made up, and she must have been at least a Level 3 because her hair was so straight there was no way she didn't have curling iron privileges. I could tell she wanted to talk, but I really just wanted to get to my room, so after I glanced up at her I rolled myself into a corner and held the MMPI test an inch from my face, like I couldn't read the print.

Despite my wheelchair moves, the woman walked in front of me and introduced herself as Ally. She asked me if it was my first time in. I pulled the paper a little bit back from my head and nodded *yes*, thinking that she'd at least take my lack of words as an indication that I didn't want to talk.

"Did you come in through the Emergency Room?" Ally continued.

I nodded again.

"I bet you got stuck in the Seclusion Room, didn't you?"

Nod.

She laughed and pulled a pack of Marlboro Lights from her pocket. A sister smoking Marlboro Lights? That almost always means she went to a predominantly white college. Suddenly, I became a little more interested in Ally—Did she go to Penn, too?—but I was still too tired to care much.

"I hate that Seclusion Room. It's so boring," Ally continued. "Next time they try to stick you in there, tell them you're claustrophobic. They'll put you in a regular room. It's worked every time for me."

Next time? Did I look that crazy?

"There won't be a next time," I said, laughing a little, trying to sound confident, even though I was in a wheelchair with a stack of psychosis forms in my lap. "I'm getting out of here in three days," I added. I'd read on one of the forms that they could keep me involuntarily for only seventy-two hours.

Ally's lips curled up in a slightly condescending smile. "Well, good luck with that. I'm going on a smoke break."

Who did she think she was laughing at? Was Ally going to be the first chick I had to fight in here? I didn't say 'bye to her, so I guess she took my silence as her cue to stand up and leave. Before getting buzzed through the double doors, she looked back at me and said, "Just get through it. Do everything they say to do, exactly how they say to do it."

In hindsight, had I listened to her, things would have been much easier. It seemed so weird for someone to be so confident about surviving the mental health system. What a horrible thing even to admit having knowledge about, especially for a black woman, I thought.

I would soon find out that Ally had been in this hospital five times before. When her medication worked, she was a high-paid budget analyst fluent in Obijwa and Italian. When it didn't work, she thought Obijwa spies were out to get her and could be found running barefoot through the city. To me, she was just a crazy person I didn't want to know. I was viewing mental illness as a cold. If I stayed away from all things related to it, Ally included, I could free myself, go back to college, and get on with my life.

I only had seventy-two hours to get through. I was going to prove I didn't need their medications or their therapies. I wouldn't eat dinner off a stupid tray or talk to a white guy I didn't know about my childhood. We all have problems, I thought. How dare I think I have the luxury of being depressed?

With the last question finished, I was shown to my room. While unpacking the few things the police had let me gather, I planned out how I would talk to no one during the seventy-two hours I was stuck behind the locked doors.

Wednesday, 8 A.M.: 58 hours to go.

Getting out of bed felt like trying to dig myself out of my own grave.

My body seemed to be made out of cinder blocks. As I lay in the bed unable to move, I daydreamed about situations that could force me to get up. *Would you get up if there was a fire?* No. *If a burglar was climbing through your window?* Nope. *If God was in your kitchen?* No, but I'd yell at him from the bed. "Hey, God, what is the point of depression? I mean, maybe it was cool to take a break like this when you first made man and we were living in gardens and eating fruit, but we're a society of productivity now. If I can't even get up to punch the clock, I might as well be dead."

I tried negative self-talk, sometimes yelling out loud like an abusive high school football coach. "Is that the best you can do? You'll never succeed in life if you let a bed beat you!"

Lying in the bed on the psych unit, unable to use God, fire, or my full bladder as a catalyst to stand upright, the only other reason I saw to get up was food.

When food is free, I feel a primal competitiveness for it, even if I'm not hungry, I can't allow someone else to get it. I knew that was partly why I weighed almost two hundred pounds. Food is more than food to me. It's what I put in my mouth when I don't want to curse anyone out, it's my nonjudgmental friend when I find out my boyfriend is cheating and using my car to do it, but dammit I'm going to stick with him because what else kind of boyfriend is a two-hundred-pound girl going to get?

You're locked up in the psychiatric ward, honey. There are more important issues at hand than free food, the sane part of my brain said. Alas, free food was the only possible reason I saw to get up.

After I lay in bed and stared up to the ceiling for over an hour, a nurse's aide came by to make sure I hadn't killed myself. I told her I hadn't. "You better get out there before someone snatches your breakfast," she said.

The horror! I pleaded with her to let me eat in my room. She said no, I had to eat with everyone else; if I didn't, I'd have a hard time convincing my doctor that I was well enough to be released.

She left to make sure my next-door neighbor hadn't committed suicide and I pulled the covers over my head. I kept thinking how someone was going to take my food and how that was more important than God to me right then. Food is real; I'm not sure God is. I rolled around on the mattress like my hands and feet were bound with duct tape. I ran out of energy and hoped that the blankets would just rise up like an angel of death and smother me.

Free food. Free food. Someone might be eating mine.

I rolled one more time and managed to separate myself from the bed. When my feet hit the floor I felt like screaming, "Woo-hoo! I just got out of bed! What's my name?" But only people who have been this depressed would understand the joy of performing a simple task like getting out of bed.

Left foot, right foot. Walk toward the free hospital food. Oh, my God, look at my life; I'm on a mental ward convincing myself to walk because there is free food at the end of the journey. *Don't think about that, just keep walking. You're almost to the cafeteria.*

I grabbed my tray and chose a seat in the corner with my back against the wall. It's a seating tactic I learned in Nation of Islam Lite—you can see everyone and no one can sneak up on you. It's supposed to be used during race riots, but I figured I could co-opt it for the mental ward cafeteria.

I watched the geriatric patients being pushed up to the tables by nurses' assistants. Anna, one of the women from last night, looked at her tray and moaned loudly. "This is horrible, just horrible!"

"Oh, shush already and eat your food," a fellow senior citizen responded from across the room. Ally entered the cafeteria and waved to me but sat with a group of college-age patients. That group included Arielle the Anorexic, who cried while she ate. A nurse stood over her shoulder throughout the whole meal, encouraging her to take "just one more bite." As soon as the nurse decided she'd eaten enough, Arielle jumped up and started power walking the length of the hall to burn the calories off.

As I poked a fork through the paper covering of my single-serving cereal bowl, a woman with stringy hair and too much nervous energy entered the cafeteria. Her eyes darted around the room and locked on mine before I could look away. She made a beeline to the seat across from me, setting her tray down like it had the weight of the world on it. She seated herself in the same manner. I gave her a quick acknowledgment smile. She took that as her cue to launch into full manic conversation.

"I told my family that I didn't want any more rabbits for presents," she said, holding direct eye contact with me.

"I was featured in the local newspaper, the county one—me, Audrey—for my rabbit collection," she said, as if that would have made me understand her first sentence.

"Every goddamn present I opened was a rabbit," she said, peeling the cover off her Rice Krispies bowl and placing a shaky hand around her juice carton. She raised the carton to her lips but, unable to steady her hand, let most of the juice dribble onto her thin hospital robe.

"It's the medication side effects," she offered, noticing me looking at her hand. "I sent out a mass e-mail to everyone, months ahead of my birthday. Do not buy me any more rabbits, I said. That period of my life is over. I'm a lawyer, for God's sake, I shouldn't collect rabbits. But every box I unwrapped had a rabbit. I got rabbit bookends, rabbit slippers, a book on taking care of rabbits even though I don't own a real rabbit, a musical figurine of a rabbit on a rocking horse that plays 'Rockabye Rabbit Baby'—"

I listened as she rattled off several dozen more rabbit items and then told me the movie-length version of her life and how she came to be here. "Once you've been in here, anytime you raise your voice, people want to call the cops. I have a right to be mad about all those rabbits, so I screamed at everyone I was going outside and then the cops came."

The rest of her story sounded like a weird sci-fi Easter tale, but I listened more intently than I had ever listened to a professor. I was fascinated. This was the most real (if one-sided) conversation I'd had in a long time. In the "sane" world, people hold back their psychotic parts. "Sane" people give you little happy bits of themselves, then months down the line when they know you're invested in their well-being/in love/committed to being their best friend, they dump their huge, crazy psychotic backstories on you, leaving you no choice but to help carry them. Sometimes, when their load gets really heavy, you think in the back of your mind, "I wish I'd known this shit earlier," but you keep trudging along with them because that's what a good friend/wife/worker does. I prefer the crazy version of friendship.

"Is it so hard to understand that I have grown out of rabbits?" Audrey continued.

Wouldn't life be easier if we all had to lay our bunnies on the table in the first conversation and say, *Take me or leave me?* We can't because we're all competing: for a job, for a man, for the Most Black Person Award. I got tired keeping all those secrets inside. I guess that's why I am here, I thought. I showed people who had no connection to me how crazy I'd been feeling on the inside. I've got to get better at holding it in, like normal people do.

Suddenly, Audrey stopped talking and dropped her head. Big tears started plopping into her cereal. She didn't try to sniffle them up; they poured out. Her Rice Krispies started crackling from the wetness. My eyes welled up, too. I wanted to say, *I understand, I understand.* I wanted to hug her. Instead, I looked around, embarrassed, wondering if anyone was judging me as weak for crying. I dabbed at my eyes with my napkin and attempted a fake sneeze that came out a little too loud to be real.

I'm crying with a white girl who collects rabbits, I thought, and that made me want to cry even more.

10 A.M.: *56 hours to go.*

There was a knock on my door. A tiny woman entered with a tape recorder and a small cardboard box tucked under her arm, squinting as though the fluorescent lights in my room were too bright. She walked over to me and extended her palm. Her hand was cold and pale, but her grip was firm, like she was letting me know she was in charge. She introduced herself as Anne and told me she was a Penn PhD student. "Your doctor asked me to administer the Thematic Apperception and Rorschach tests to you," she said, setting her tape recorder down on the dresser. Unlike the manic woman from the cafeteria, Anne barely looked me straight in the eye; she seemed unsettled. I wondered if she was unsure of herself or afraid of me. I wondered if she knew I went to Penn also and she was picturing herself lying where I was.

As Anne was arranging her cards and fiddling with her tape recorder, she dropped both the box of cards and the tape recorder on the floor. I noticed a battery rolling near my foot, so I started to lean over to stop it. Anne, who was also chasing the battery, jumped back when she saw me lean forward. *Oh, God, they've sent me a racist test administrator.*

I hate covert racism. I have always hated guessing whether someone is being mean/rude/nervous because they hate my race or because they are having a bad day. As I got older, I noticed that covert racism is just like depression: You know it when you feel it, but it's hard to explain to someone who has never experienced it. It's like a sixth sense that God has given people of color that white people don't believe in. *We just know.* Unfortunately, I couldn't just come straight out and ask Anne if she was afraid of blacks because (1) people don't tend to talk about racism and (2) I could have gotten accused of playing the race card. I was wishing it were the 1950s. If it were, she could have just said, "I don't want to test a nigger."

Time to play Put the White Woman at Ease, I thought. Put the White Woman at Ease (a.k.a. PuWWE or PU, for short) is what my friends and I had taken to calling this phenomenon. PU is the ultimate passive response to racism. It's more passive than turning the other cheek; it's *work your ass off to prove you're smart/not a thief/ polite/not as crazy as the intake sheet says* so you can change this white woman's mind about all black people. It's my Boonie neighbors and their "Don't let white people see you acting like that" threats. It's me buying the most expensive item on a store shelf just to spite the saleswoman, who acts like I am poor black trash who obviously can't afford anything in the boutique. I might not have enough money to get home after that, but *dammit I showed her.* And people wonder why there are black folks on the bus with a car's worth of diamonds in their ears. Those diamonds were probably a result of PU—showing some saleswoman they weren't a thief.

I sat back up and let Anne get her own damn battery.

"Would you feel safer if I were strapped in a wheelchair?" I asked.

She paused like she was seriously considering my question. "No, you're fine on the bed," she said.

Anne sat down and started explaining the Thematic Apperception Test (TAT) to me. "Basically, the TAT is a storytelling game. I'm going to hold up a drawing and you tell me a story about it."

Yay. Fun.

Anne held up the first card, a pencil drawing of a boy sitting near a violin. Why would a boy sit near a violin and not play it? I wondered.

"The pencil-drawn boy is mad because he really wants to play the drums. He doesn't see anyone on MTV playing the violin. He's a virgin, and he knows carrying a violin case to school will not help him get laid," I said, purposefully trying to keep my sentences simple but entertaining.

"Mmmmhmmm," Anne murmured intermittently, while jotting down notes. Does any mental health professional realize how hard it is to give honest responses when someone is taking notes? All I could focus on was that she was going to write down whatever I said and it would be in some file forever. I was extremely conscious of every word.

Anne revealed the next card. It was a pencil drawing chockful of white people. As were the third, fourth, fifth, and sixth cards. All the images on the cards seemed inherently sad. I couldn't pinpoint if it was because not one drawing so far had featured a smiling person on the cards or that, to me, black-and-white pencil drawings were inherently sad.

I looked up at the seventh card, which had white people lounging on a back porch with what looked like cotton fields stretched out before them.

"What year was this test developed?" I asked, thinking that only a die-hard racist would subject mentally ill black people to a test full of scowling white people on a plantation.

"The TAT was developed in the nineteen-thirties," Anne replied.

"Are there any black people on these cards?"

"No."

Was this really the best modern medicine could do, multiple-choice questions and quizzes made during the Great Depression? They had that at the fucking DMV.

Of course, I didn't say that out loud. If my reaching for her battery made Anne jump, I'm sure a curse word would have sent her punching at the panic button on my wall. I reworded what I was thinking and said it in a PU way, a way that proved I was smart.

"So, if I had come in with two bad kidneys, doctors could pull one out of my brother and send me home. I come in with my brain supposedly broken, the part of my body that controls all the other parts, and the best I get are picture tests?"

"These tests are very accurate in diagnosing. . . ."

Stop regurgitating what your professor told you and think! I wanted to scream. *If you were depressed and I showed you cards full of black people, you'd probably scare yourself out of your depression.*

I wanted to curse Anne out in ways she'd only seen on television. Some people are angry drunks; I'm an angry depressive. I got so mad that this fog had chosen to invade my brain, there was no stopping me when I was set off. Luckily for me and the physical health of the people around me, my weapon of choice is my mouth. I have avoided being mugged by using my smart mouth when I wasn't depressed; when I am depressed, I could end up taking the muggers' money. I wanted to unleash every ounce of my pent-up anger toward women who looked like this one, women who had never had to live in a world where even the tests designed to help them get well don't have their kind of people in them.

Be calm. Find a nice PU way to deal with your anger. The ends justify the means. The end is escape; you need to get out of here.

"Can I make some of these people black, or will that lower my score?" I asked.

Anne told me there was no score.

Great, let's move on.

The next card featured a woman sitting on a bed; her head was in her hands. A man stood in the foreground of the sketch, looking angry and staring out into space. The room in the sketch seemed too sterile to be a loving home, so I decided they were in a hotel. I named the man Ike and the woman Tina, as they were, in my mind, black and those were the first names I thought of.

I told Anne that Tina was sad because she got a horrible prize on *The Price Is Right*. She won a patio set, but unfortunately she and Ike lived in an apartment in Detroit and it barely had a working bathroom, let alone a place for a patio set—a set that would cost almost a thousand dollars to ship back home to Detroit. Ike and Tina didn't even know anyone who had a patio. Tina wondered if the set would look good in the living room; she'd have to find someone to take the umbrella. Ike was mad at Tina because Tina convinced him to use their savings and take vacation time to be on *The Price Is Right*. He was also irritated that Tina wouldn't stop asking him if she appeared disappointed when Bob said she would be playing Cliff Hangers. Tina was only asking him because she didn't want to look ungrateful on national television. What would the church folks say if she did? A lot of people in their church would have killed to have a patio set.

I liked my story. I started laughing.

"Mmmhmmm," Anne responded.

Mmmhmmm, what, bitch? I wanted to say. Mmmhmmm, she's crazy, or Mmmhmmm, I too wonder what people who live in Detroit apartments do when they win patio sets on *The Price Is Right*? My anger was growing because I'd barely had enough energy to get up that morning and I was getting tired of this PU and being a shining example of my race all because she got scared of my trying to pick up a battery.

Twenty cards later, when my mouth was desert-dry from all the stories, Anne pulled out the Rorschach. I told her every photo looked like a squashed bug except for the last one, which looked like a man with a lasso or a baby falling from an umbilical cord. I told her the umbilical cord one to let her know I was smart and knew the word *umbilical*. The word probably popped into my mind because, the week before, my mother had told me about a doctor she worked with who made fun of the black babies' exotic names and had suggested the name Umbilical to one new mother. Not knowing the meaning and not wanting to offend the doctor, the lady had agreed that Umbilical was a nice name. After the doctor left, my mother had had to tell the new mother that the doctor was making fun of her.

Finally, Anne let me know the test was over and she'd give the results to my doctor tomorrow morning. I exhaled.

"I can't wait," I said, very seriously.

Thursday, 8 A.M.: 34 hours to go.

My doctor, Dr. Chase, and his team woke me. The doctor asked how I was feeling. His interns' pens stood at attention, ready to take down every word my crazy mouth said.

"Better," I replied. I wasn't lying. Better than when I came in, but not good enough to be fine. The students in the semicircle around my bed started writing on their notepads.

All I said was better. Why are they writing a manifesto?

The doctor noticed my open notebook on the nightstand, took a look at the material, and said, "You're studying some hard stuff there."

Be normal, be normal, be normal! Say something normal so you can leave.

"I'm really worried about missing my classes. If I miss this se-mester, I won't have any money to continue," I said, knowing damn well that I was not going to go to a single class. I was going to crawl right back into my bed at home. At least it was my bed.

He told me I should stay and give the treatments a chance. He thought I was seriously depressed, he said. I told him I felt good enough to leave today and I actually had just had an overreaction and I was not going to kill myself. I didn't tell him it was all a mis-understanding. Normal people take responsibility.

He said if he couldn't convince me to stay, he'd have the nurse bring forms for me to fill out.

"You'll be signing out against medical advice, but I have to tell you, most patients who do that end up back here within a week."

I told him I doubted if I'd be back, but I'd reconsider if they got some black people on the Thematic Apperception Test. His interns began scribbling notes again. I imagined that they were writing Jane Doe, BF, 21, leaving because there are no Negroes on our testing materials.

"Do you want a copy of your TAT results?" He opened his folder and held three sheets of stapled paper out to me.

I began reading the analysis. "Angela's responses reveal a preoccupation with issues of race and physical appearance."

Because I made some people black on their all-white test meant I was preoccupied with race? They needed to diagnose the testmaker as being preoccupied with the white race for not putting any black folks in the test.

Reading the results made me even more anxious to sign out against medical advice. I didn't want to read any more. I folded the rest of the test results up and placed them in my pocket.

Before leaving to check on his next patient, Dr. Chase wrote me a prescription for Prozac and wished me well. His interns wished me nothing, at least not out loud. All of them walked through my door looking down at their pads, still writing notes.

I had few things to pack, but it took me an hour to gather the energy to move from my bed. When I steeled myself to face the outside world, I went to the nurses' station to retrieve my one hazardous item (earrings). Ally was sitting there playing cards. "Do you want to play Spades before Cognitive Therapy?" she asked.

I smiled down at her. "I'd love to, but I'm leaving," I replied, putting in my contraband earrings. "Told you," I added as the bulletproof doors opened. I turned and walked through them like I was gliding down a catwalk, trying my best to blend in with the normal people.

Friday 8 P.M.: 10 hours of freedom. Nation of Islam Lite meeting.
For two hours before the meeting I sat in my apartment trying to figure out a way to get help from the conscious brothers and sisters without saying the word *depressed*. I finally settled on *sluggish*.

"Does anyone have any recommendations for herbalists who deal with extreme, severe, desperate sluggishness?" I asked.

A grad student, Isis, gave me the name of a woman who was an herbalist as well as an iridologist.

"Makeba is good. She can tell your life story, your energy, and all your illnesses from looking at your eyes," Isis told me.

Saturday, 10 A.M.: 24 hours of freedom.

Makeba greeted me with a stare so hard, so stiff, I half expected a computer printout to come from her mouth. Seriously, if you're going to greet someone by staring, at least tell her what you see. She freaked me out; I was way too scared to tell her I needed herbs for depression, plus if she didn't see it in my eyes, I must not have really needed any.

"I need herbs—for a rash," I said, when she asked what I came for.

"Where is the rash?" she asked, still scanning my eyes.

"Between my legs," I replied.

Damn, that's what I got for not being honest and telling her what I really needed. Now she would think I have VD. What are you supposed to do when someone stares at you and doesn't look away? It's abnormal to stare at people; that's why we have contests to see who can stare longest without blinking. I did have a rash between my legs, but it was on my upper inner thighs and it was just because I was fat and my legs rubbed together when I walked.

She started reaching for her tincture bottles. I needed to speak up before she mixed some Herpes-B-Gone concoction and called Isis to tell her I was burning. "The rash isn't really bad. It's between my legs on my thighs."

She stopped shuffling the herb bottles. "A thigh rash? Do you know what caused it?"

"My other thigh," I replied, very seriously.

She almost laughed, but stopped herself by focusing on my eyes again. I heard buzzing and clicking noises coming from her brain.

"Have you tried putting Band-Aids on your inner thighs when you wear skirts?" she asked, looking down at my thunder thighs. It didn't take an iridologist to tell me I was overweight and Band-Aids would stop the chafe. I had read that tip on an online weight-loss message board.

Just tell her you're depressed, I thought, but instead, I thanked her for the Band-Aid suggestion and bought some spirulina because she said it might help me lose weight.

The spirulina was of no use to me because I couldn't OD on it, so I threw it out as soon as I got around the corner. Instead of going back to school, I walked ten blocks back to the hospital.

Saturday, noon: One minute left of freedom.

I walked into the Emergency Room and told the receptionist that I was just on the psych unit and needed to go back. When I got back up to my floor, I shoved my tail between my legs and swallowed my pride. It was like breaking up with a man, calling him a piece of shit, and then realizing he's the best man out there and having to beg for him to take you back. My bed was still open; I was the last discharge and the newest admit.

Mentally ill people are the most forgiving bunch of people I've ever met. "We've all done it. Welcome back. Don't touch me!" Rose with the combination dementia/Alzheimer's said.

Her white old-lady friends actually hugged me. "Give it a shot," Mary said, then sat down and told me she tried to bite a doctor the first time she was committed.

I apologized to Ally for dissing her. She snuck her curling iron into my room for the next two days, and then she was discharged.

The only person I wanted to stay away from was Gus, a tall white guy who was always a little jumpy, like he was high. He swore he was the don of the psych ward, telling anyone who would listen about how much money he had and how he could do whatever he wanted because he paid cash for his treatment.

Rose and her circle of old ladies became my primary hanging partners. Not that I'd had a change of opinion about white people but I only had energy for old people. They didn't want much—mostly, just someone to listen to them—and that's all I had to give.

My fourth night back, I was sitting there watching *Beverly Hills Cop* with them and Gus sat uncomfortably close to me on the couch. "I'd like to stick a banana in your tailpipe," he said, modeling a very vulgar come-on line after a scene in the movie.

"Could you get away from me?" I asked. He looked shocked, got up, and walked into the kitchen.

"He's a real asshole," Rose offered.

Gus came back chomping on a Saltine, with crumbs falling out of his mouth. He sat so close to me again he was rubbing up against my arm. I asked him once to stop. He moved away for a second, then rubbed his hand up and down my arm. I pulled back and clocked the shit out of him, aiming for his eye but hitting him on his ear.

"Nurse!" he yelled, holding his ear like it would fall off if he didn't keep his palm pressed to it. "She violated the no-punching rule!"

A small female doctor ran up to me. "Sit down! Sit down!" she yelled. I started screaming at her.

"*He* rubbed up against me, yell at *him!*"

Not one patient was having a manic moment or was caught in the grip of dementia. My yelling was more captivating than any medication, any phone call, anyone Eddie Murphy was arresting on the television set.

"I said *sit down!*" she yelled.

"Of course you're not going to yell at the *white* guy! He can do whatever he wants!" I replied, refusing to sit. She ran to the phone, and soon two black security guards were buzzed through the doors toward me.

My mouth stayed on full blast. "Oh, sure, y'all do whatever the white woman says. Beat up the black woman for the white woman!" I said as they grabbed me under both arms and threw me into a restraining jacket. With me safely in the jacket, the doctor injected me with something.

When I woke up from the shot I was on another floor, locked in a room with only one window that looked out to an empty hallway. The floor was made of soft squares of padded foam. I was bored as hell, so I played hopscotch. Finally, I pounded on the door to try to get someone's attention.

"I have to go to the bathroom!" I screamed, thinking that was an ingenious way to get someone to let me out. The door opened a crack and a nurse's aide threw a plastic toilet in at me like she was throwing meat to a vicious animal. While I peed in it, I said hello to rock bottom. To this day, whenever I think I can't get through something, I ask myself if it is worse than crouching in the corner of a foam room, peeing in a plastic toilet and hoping that no one decides to peek in the small window as I do it. If the answer is no, I keep on pushing forward.

Finally, I was deemed sane enough to get out of isolation, but not sane enough to go back to the floor I was on. Because of my ear punch, I was marked more dangerous and had to stay on Floor Two, with the psychotics and the schizophrenics. No need to search for black people up on Floor Two; it was all black. When word got out that I was from Floor One and was transferred to Floor Two for punching a white guy, I was Miss Popularity.

"I heard it was mostly white down there and you had to have private insurance," my new roommate, Kay, said. "They throw the poor niggas up here."

Besides the all-black population, there were two other big differences from the level I'd come from. On Floor One, almost every patient had visitors and it wasn't uncommon for them to stay for the entire four hours they were allowed. On Floor Two, only one person had a visitor all day.

In Floor Two groups, when any of the doctors or group leaders tried to talk to the patients, they'd respond either with a shake of the head or with nothing at all. I fell right in line with the doctor-ignoring culture. I didn't want people to think I was trying to be the cute light-skinned girl making friends with the enemy. My Occupational Therapy leader sighed in frustration, as if we were beyond help.

When I got out of the psych ward and researched black people and depression, I read numerous studies that detailed rampant misdiagnosing of depression as schizophrenia among African Americans. When black people show distrust of the system, as I had, by calling out, "Of course you're not going to yell at the *white* guy," they are often labeled delusional. It's hard enough to navigate the mental health system with the right diagnosis. With the wrong diagnosis and no support from outside sources (whether your lack of visitors stems from keeping your hospitalization secret or because your family is ashamed of you), I have a hard time seeing how anyone could get better.

I didn't want to be one of those people.

What I wanted to do was get off Floor Two. I knew I couldn't do that by ignoring the group leaders and doctors, so I started talking. In morning meeting, I talked about how shitty I felt and how much I missed my cats, cringing as the other patients looked at me like I was a traitor. In Occupational Therapy, I answered every question asked. If no one interrupted me, I kept talking, certain that pouring out my soul about the emotions I felt while cutting up Jones New York ads would be my ticket to freedom.

"Your group leader thinks you're manic," Dr. Chase informed me. I cut my talking back by half.

Finally, two days later, I was allowed to go back downstairs. The official word as to why I was allowed back was that I was finally "behaving properly," but two nurses and all the old ladies told me otherwise: Rose and her friends, Mary and Elizabeth, had refused to eat until they brought me back downstairs. Three old ladies went on a hunger strike for me!

"They didn't have to straitjacket you!" Mary said.

"That was wrong. We'd been telling them for quite a while that Gus is a shit!" Elizabeth added.

I started smiling. Look at these three old white ladies with their own problems sticking up for me. They were widowed, with uncaring children, depression, and dementia, and they were sticking up for me. Maybe these frail white ladies weren't devils.

Who cares if they are? I thought. What if I just do what *I* feel like doing and not worry about how people judge me for it?

I grabbed my tray off the rack and sat with my new friends.

It seemed like such a simple thing, but I couldn't remember the last time I had done anything in front of people without fear of judgment. The uncomplicated act of sitting where I wanted to sit felt so powerful that I closed my eyes and said a silent prayer, grateful for the insanity and those three hungry old white ladies for giving me the kick start I needed.

For All My Dogs in the Hood

Census samples show that mixed marriages are more than twice as common in California—involving roughly one of every ten couples, compared to one of every twenty-five U.S. couples elsewhere—than the rest of the nation. And their rate is climbing in Los Angeles among younger adults.

—*"Mixed Unions Changing the Face of Marriage,"* Los Angeles Times, *April 28, 1998*

The temp office interviewer looked at my application. "It took you six years to graduate?" she asked.

"Yes, I took a few semesters off to save up tuition money," I said. It was a half-truth, but I'm sure if I'd added "And a few semesters for this pesky depression problem I had," she'd be screaming "Next in line, please!" faster than I could fill out my W-2 form.

After I stumbled my way through a Microsoft Excel test and cursed myself for majoring in Medical Anthropology, I had my official first job out of college. Starting Monday, I'd be assembling tax returns for the IRS.

My office was a small back room I shared with three other recent college graduates. Like me, they all searched Monster.com looking for a better gig when our supervisor left the room. Unlike me, they were all white.

It was only my second job where I was the only nonwhite person. I had gotten fired from the first job, seven years ago. Claire, a white girl I'd become friendly with, had asked me something I considered offensive while we were unpacking a new shipment of clothes.

"Can I ask you something? Exactly how much bigger are black men's dicks? I've always been curious."

I called her a nasty slut and started slamming the clothes on the racks so hard, customers stared in fear and moved to the other side of the store.

I didn't talk much to any of my coworkers after that and got a reputation as rude. After the Christmas rush, I received my pink slip.

This time, I was determined to be a team player. I sat with my colleagues at lunch and tried to join in the conversation whenever possible. Usually, it wasn't possible; I just had no point of reference for the things they talked about. My coworkers went to different bars, liked different music, and watched different television stations. "Did anyone catch *In Living Color* last night?" I'd say, to the sound of crickets chirping.

The third week of work, the lunch topic was our parents.

"My mother would drive through a hurricane to save fifteen cents," Danielle said, picking at the Band-Aids she wore on the tips of her fingers to protect her from 1040EZ paper cuts.

"My mother, too!" I said, excited at a conversation I could finally participate in. "Her favorite store was the House of Bargains. It was in a really scary neighborhood where people were burning down black people's houses. Once, this kid called me a nigger but my mother said to his mother, 'How you going to call someone a nigger when you're shopping in the House of Bargains?' Puh-lease." I laughed, doing the best imitation of my mother's voice.

When I looked at my coworkers' faces, I felt like slinking out the back door. No one laughed with me, not even the sympathy laugh that bombing comedians get. Everyone sat shifting in their seats, trying to adjust to the uncomfortable cloud of silence now hanging over our cafeteria table. Danielle finally broke the silence, and my coworkers' comments came tumbling out like dominoes.

"Oh, my God! It's like you grew up in the sixties!"

"Angela, I had no idea. I am so sorry!"

Hey, I wanted to say, didn't someone else just talk about their father passing out in a drunken stupor night after night? No one apologized for that! I felt so stupid; I was only trying to bond with my all-white coworkers instead of being stereotyped as the black girl who kept to herself. Now I was afraid that people thought I was trying to get sympathy by pulling out some dusty House of Bargains race card.

Of course, after I knew how they felt, I had to spend the next twenty minutes telling them it was all right. "Don't feel bad, Jake! You weren't the one who teased me! . . . No, Danielle, I know black women age more slowly than white women, but I'm only twenty-three. It wasn't the sixties."

Rebecca, a coworker from Missouri, asked for a list of books to read on "the black experience." Of course, I was glad she was trying to learn. God bless her. But my job wasn't to teach, it was to staple tax returns. I wasn't going to be her Black World tour guide when the African American museum was right down the street from our office. Plus, if she started asking about racial shit that got me emotional, I might lose my job again. I had already slipped up by telling everyone the House of Bargains story. I'd have to go back to being the black woman worker who kept to herself. Better cold than angry, I thought, as Rebecca asked again for a list of black experience books.

"Which black experience?" I asked, as in, Do you want to read about Clarence Thomas or Tupac?

"Just, you know, the regular one," she replied.

I forced myself to take a deep breath. How does a grown woman educated for sixteen years in private schools not know one book on the black experience (regular or irregular version) and have the same job I do? I studied European history for years. I told her I'd look into it for her and excused myself to go to the bathroom, where I exploded.

My white coworkers' mortified reactions to the House of Bargains story surprised me. Did they truly think the nation had a funeral for racism when the COLORED signs came down off the water fountains? How could people still be saying *nigger* when Martin Luther King has a holiday, for crying out loud? Which congressman can we write to, Angela? In the stall alone, I thought maybe I was being too hard on them. Maybe no one said *nigger* in their hoods in the eighties.

I was eager to get home. In the spirit of keeping it real, I had my first postcollege apartment in the hood. I wasn't going to be one of those black people who took their degrees and moved out to all-white neighborhoods in the suburbs.

After one month living there, I was definitely keeping it real—real terrified. My next-door neighbors had started a nightly ritual of shooting out streetlights from their roof. Afraid of getting a bullet in the brain, I started sleeping on the floor.

Instead of rushing home to get away from the white people, I was begging to hang out with them after work.

"You know, I've always wanted to go to a grunge concert," I lied to Danielle.

After weeks of hanging out listening to music I hated, only to come home to sleep near the litter box, I decided to make a major change. I was leaving Philly.

For a single black (somewhat) professional, Philly started to feel like a small town. There were only one or two black professional–friendly hangouts and, like every other major city, half as many professional black men as black women. After a year of happy hours, I went into the bar and realized I'd dated every man there.

I guess Philly also seemed like a small town because I'd been part of all of it, from the acute level of the psych ward to the most expensive private school. It all had been adding up to way too many intimate encounters for me. There's only so many times you can walk out of your new temp tax-return job with your business suit and your white colleagues and be greeted by name by the homeless guy. "Bitch, don't act new," he said. "You know you were up in the hospital with me."

"I *worked* in the hospital with you," I'd lie, hoping my colleagues couldn't see my lip quivering.

My girlfriends were moving safe distances away like Jersey and Washington, DC, I wanted to go to California. My psychiatrist said I seemed to have seasonal affective disorder. I wanted some sun.

"It's dangerous out in LA," a black secretary at my job warned me.

"The cops whip black people's behinds for jaywalking," my grandmother said.

Without fail, every black person would warn me not to wear red or blue once my plane touched down at LAX. "There's no light-skinned or dark-skinned out there, just red and blue," my girl-friend said.

Sounded good to me.

"Are you sure you want to give up that job with benefits?" my mother asked me. "People would kill to have a temp job that covers two dentist visits a year."

My entire family lives in the Philly area, and moving across country with only a bunch of savings and a need for change seemed irrational to my mother.

"And you're not moving for love?" my mother asked, remembering when I was in high school and would have moved to Mars if a boy told me he loved me. I assured her that I was definitely not moving for love. If I had half the sex life now that I had in high school, I would definitely be staying in Philly, I thought. The best romance I'd had recently was with a self-tortured artist who lived 120 miles away in Maryland. I'd drive four hours just to sit on his twin bed, rub his back, and convince him that stress wasn't enough to rupture his colon, but even if it did, I'd push him and his colostomy bag wherever he needed to go. His mom would come in and tell him his underwear was washed and ask did he want his favorite food for dinner. He was twenty-six. Thank God he broke my heart.

My mother gave up questioning my motives until the day she drove me to Goodwill to donate almost every piece of clothing I owned. I still had six months before my planned move, but I was slowly getting rid of everything. I wanted to move to California with no baggage, mental or physical.

"Angela, I have to say, if it's the crazy homeless man outside your office who's making you do this, there are other ways of dealing with him," she said, and went on to tell me how I could get him involuntarily committed, just like the police had done to me. "I wouldn't feel right if I didn't tell you that I think moving to Los Angeles alone is foolish."

"Mom, Jesus did a lot of things people believed to be foolish," I said, and immediately wished I could suck the words back into my mouth. My mother knew I still didn't love Jesus as much as she did, even though, out of respect, I'd ceased calling him "the Christian God the white man uses to control you."

I didn't want to tell my mother the real reason and start dredging up the past. Talking about all the mistakes I'd made in this city, including the latest one, moving to the hood, trying to make a difference. The only difference I'd made so far was asking my landlord to install a deadbolt.

I didn't feel like explaining to her that I was trying to make up for all the time I'd wasted hating white people in college. I remember that during my first semester a Black History professor told me that many black nationalists go through a "hating white people phase." In response, I laughed out loud. A phase? *Please.* At the time, I thought that hate, much like teal, was a great color on me. I could never see giving it up.

Nevertheless, there comes a time in every hater's life when the antidepressants kick in and she sees that hate hasn't done a damn thing for her, nor has it prodded her to do anything for anyone else. I wasn't even that good at hating. At least the KKK has marches; all I did was go to the tanning salon and watch a bunch of taped lectures.

I was ashamed. I had learned a lot more in Nation of Islam Lite than why white people were worthy of my hate. I had also become aware of how much better I had it than the majority of black people. Sometime during my senior year I promised myself that when I graduated and got a job, I'd move into the hood and start planning that Black History school I used to talk about with Mah.

So, I'd done it. I'd moved smack dab into the middle of the hood. And just like my plan to move to Los Angeles, some black people thought I was crazy. My ex-boyfriend's mother, a black Washington, DC, socialite, told me over dinner that I didn't owe black people a damn thing. The harshness of her response jarred me. Flustered, I squeaked back, "Well, people helped me out, and I just want to do the same thing." She huffed, refilled her champagne flute, and sat in silence for the rest of the dinner, like she wasn't wasting her words on an Ivy League dunce who wanted to squander her life by living in the ghetto.

If I told my mother the truth about what finally pushed me to buy the plane tickets to LA, that my teenage next-door neighbor had recently threatened to kill me, she'd swear we could solve this by having a sit-down with his mother. Unfortunately, Gene carried guns. His mother probably did, too.

The only time I heard Gene's mother talk to him was when she yelled about how bad he was at selling weed. At least twice a week, she'd scream that if he couldn't do better at selling weed, maybe he should think about getting his dumb ass back into school. I could hear their conversations because only a small alley separated our ground-floor apartments, and neither of us had air-conditioning so our windows were always open, trying to catch a hot South Philly breeze. You could hear everything. Sometimes, I even heard his shower running.

Two months earlier, Gene had bought his sister Janet a pit bull puppy for her thirteenth birthday. I watched their backyard party from my window. When Gene held up the energetic puppy, he was the hit of the party. After blowing out her candles, Janet kissed her puppy and announced, "By the time I'm fourteen, I'm gonna have made so much money fighting this li'l motherfucker!"

Oh, my goodness, I thought. She's the same lost teenager that I was. Next time I see her outside, I'm going to tell her that young women don't need to fight puppies to be beautiful.

Two weeks passed and I hadn't talked to her. It was nearing April 15 and I was stapling tax returns from 8 A.M. until midnight every weekday. On weekends, I made excuses about why I couldn't talk to her: *I need me time,* or *I haven't seen my mother in a while.* Truth is, I was scared of Janet. I was scared she could whup my ass like she was Christina and Tascha's protégée and that her brother would back her up with one of his new pistols.

At that point, the puppy pretty much lived alone in the backyard. My apartment building was longer than Gene's, so my bedroom was right next to the yard.

One morning when I woke up for work, I heard Gene stomping around and screaming. "That was my blunt, motherfucker!" he yelled, and stormed into the backyard. He snatched the puppy up and took him inside. Two minutes of yelling about an eaten marijuana wrapper were followed by what sounded like a belt snapping and the little puppy's yelp.

I couldn't just lie in bed while a puppy cried for help. One of my grand hood plans was to start a public school program that brought animals back into the classroom. Of course all these kids treated animals poorly. They'd never had the experience of the unconditional love a pet gives, I thought as I started writing requests for funding plans I never got around to finishing. When I heard that puppy yelp, I wanted to throw a boot through Gene's window and hit him in the head. *God, I hope my hunch that abusers are reincarnated as victims is accurate.* Unfortunately, I didn't have the patience to wait for Gene's afterlife karma to kick in. I had to do something to save the puppy.

The puppy yelped again. I hopped out of bed buck naked and

ducked under the windowsill. As soon as I made sure all of my easily identifiable curls were tucked under the ledge, I screamed into the alley, "Stop beating the dog, you little punk bitch!"

There was a brief moment of silence from Gene's side; then he yelled, "Who the fuck is that?"

For some reason, I kept going. "Stop hitting the dog and hit a man your size! Or are you a fucking punk who hits dogs?"

Yes, that's me. Ivy League grad bringing peace to the hood.

The thought of Gene scared and confused gave me confidence, so I yelled again in the deepest voice I could muster. "I see you don't have shit to say now. Stop hitting the dog. Be a man and hit some shit that can hit back!" I crouched a little lower after I yelled that. I was afraid something might come crashing through the window.

Gene responded to my demand with "Shut the fuck up! If I find out who you are, I'm-a fuck you up!" I heard the sound of a gun cocking.

My nose was pressed into the carpet. I was certain Gene was going to run to his building's roof and aim at my window until he saw blood splatter against it. My thoughts were spinning. How will I ever leave my house? Does Gene know my voice? I don't think I've ever spoken to him; I only nod when I walk by. Of course, he knows I live in the building next door to his, but I don't think he knows that I live on the ground floor. Doesn't God protect those who look after small creatures? Isn't that like a beatitude or something? Yes, God won't let me die. He wants me to save the puppy. Having convinced myself, I crawled to my bathroom to get in the shower.

But then I thought, What if Gene gets even madder that someone yelled at him and takes it out on the dog? What if he kills the dog? I couldn't live with that. More action had to be taken. I crawled against the linoleum floor and, still too scared to stand upright, I threw shoes at the wall phone until it dropped into my hands. I dialed the SPCA.

The woman who answered the SPCA hotline sounded like she weighed about ninety pounds and put a fresh flower in her hair on weekends before attending peace rallies. She made sentences that weren't questions sound like questions. "Thanks for calling the SPCA?" She took my complaint and asked for my name and number. I asked her twice if the SPCA was going to tell Gene that I complained. She replied, "No, we wouldn't do that?" I wished she were a little more sure of herself. I knew she'd never lived next to a drug dealer. I warily gave her my correct contact information in hopes that it would just be used to ensure that I, the complainer, was a real person and that they would take the call more seriously knowing that. She told me they would send someone to Gene's house ("So, we'll be sending someone to that house?"). I didn't believe her.

Shame on me. The SPCA proved to be street-smart. Three days later I got a call from a guy who sounded like Barry White. Barry told me he'd visited Gene. God bless the SPCA for having diversity training, I thought. I was hoping the flower-wearing hotline woman didn't go out on calls. Sending a meek-sounding librarian to Gene's house would have been about as effective as sending two kissing Latino men in to follow up on a complaint that seventy-five guys were burning a cross in my backyard.

I imagined this mysterious SPCA man to be tall, with skin as rich in color as his voice. I wondered if he was single or if I'd already met him at the bar. I hoped that as soon as Gene opened the door to him, Gene realized that SPCA Brother was the father he'd never had but the one he needed, a tough and stern dad but one who used his big hands only to rescue little animals. I loved SPCA Brother. I pledged to be rich so I could send checks to the SPCA.

SPCA Brother told me he'd schooled Gene on the proper care of a puppy but couldn't remove the puppy from the house as it had no outward signs of abuse. SPCA Brother told me that he'd left Gene with mandatory pamphlets and informed Gene that his neighbors had turned him in.

"Oh, my God! You told him I turned him in?"

"No, of course not. I told him we were responding to the complaints of a neighbor."

I wanted to believe SPCA Brother, what with a voice that

sounded more suited to removing panties than rescuing puppies, but I felt in my gut that somehow drug-dealin' Gene knew I was the snitch. My sixth sense was confirmed the next afternoon when I saw Gene outside. He barked at me.

I couldn't believe he'd barked at me. I tried to play cool and nodded my head at him like I always did but I'm sure my first look was surprise. I would have been prepared for Gene to shoot me but not to bark. Was that a new greeting I wasn't up on? I knew I shouldn't have stopped watching *106th and Park.*

The next day, Gene was on the porch with a friend. He barked at me again. "Man, you need to stop messing with her," his friend said, laughing.

I went into my apartment and kept the blinds down. I had to figure out a way to let Gene know I wasn't the SPCA snitch.

The next evening, I came up with a plan before I rounded the corner. Right before I hit my block, I started having a pretend conversation on my cell phone. I talked loudly, with a Jamaican accent. I'd learned the accent when a woman who ran the Campus Curry food truck swore up and down that I looked like I was from the islands. I had taken that identity on for a while, dropping the *h* sound from all my words. *Ain't not'ing but a 'ting. . . .*

I was certain being Jamaican would solve the Gene problem. The woman yelling out of the window at him when he was hitting the puppy was American; I'm his neighbor Angie from Kingston. I thanked God for my chameleon-like abilities.

"Mi rada you no talk to mi!" I yelled into my mouthpiece, trying to replicate what the Campus Curry chef said when her boyfriend tried to win her back after she found out he was cheating with a white girl. "Blond 'airs were all over mi 'ouse," she told me while she cooked my codfish.

My accent threw Gene off a bit. I felt him stare, but he didn't bark. After I was safely in my apartment, I congratulated myself by listening to "No Woman, No Cry." I found an online guide to speaking patois and studied it as intently as if I had only a day to learn basic French before going to Paris.

The next evening I had a date with this guy Rob. It was my first date in two months, so I was determined to keep this budding relationship alive. The week up to our date, I read *The Rules* every night and chanted "do not sleep with him, do not sleep with him" every morning. *If he asks to come in after the date, do not let him.*

As we were turning the corner to my block, Rob asked if he could come upstairs and use my bathroom. I saw Gene coming out of his apartment. I had no choice but to answer Rob in patois.

Shit. How do you say *My toilet is broken* in patois? "Me kyann pee indoor," I replied instead.

Rob looked at me like *Who is this woman?* I must have looked like I had multiple personality disorder. I hadn't told him about Gene during dinner. I mean, what kind of conversation would that be? *By the way, if you decide to walk me home, Gene the drug-dealing puppy-beater might be outside, so I'll have to start talking like I'm from Jamaica, okay? Can you order an apple-tini for me? I'm going to run to the restroom.*

The look on Rob's face said it all anyway. He didn't want to come in after hearing me talk in a Jamaican accent about peeing indoors. He didn't say *What?* or ask for clarification or anything. He just walked me through the main entrance to my apartment door, said, "Good night," and walked away. I was glad Gene had seen him escort me in, though. Before that, he'd never seen a man at my door.

I waited five minutes before calling Rob on his cell phone to explain my sudden lapse into patois. He picked up on the second ring.

"I'm glad you called. I thought maybe you had a thing with your next-door neighbor," Rob said.

"What? What the hell are you talking about?" I asked, shocked at the mention of my next-door neighbor.

"Damn, calm down, I was just kidding. I should think you don't mess with teenagers." I wanted to strangle Rob through the phone. I felt like my heart was pounding into my throat.

"He does have a crush on you, though. He said I was lucky to have an island girl and asked what island you were from."

My heart began double-pumping and I started to sweat.

"And what did you tell him?" I screamed, even though I knew I should have been whispering. If Gene was in his apartment, he could probably hear my whole conversation.

"Damn, what is wrong with you? I'm not telling you anything if you don't stop yelling," Rob said.

I agreed only because I needed to hear the rest of the story to know whether I needed to pack my shit and go right away.

"I told him you were from a part of Jamaica called Southwest Philly," Rob said, and chuckled. Oh, so Rob's a comedian now? I should have known he thought he was funny when he touched my suede skirt before dinner and asked, "Is this felt? Well, it is now." Who does he think he is, making jokes to Gene about me?

Rob was probably afraid of Gene's thug act, the way he leaned against the wall outside like he built it and spat on the ground like he was marking his turf via saliva, so he said something to try to make him laugh. I know all about using humor to shield yourself from people you think can kill you. That's partially how I got myself through junior high. But Rob had no right to tell Gene where I was from.

"Well, Robert. Congratulations. You just killed your date." I said this slowly and calmly, enunciating each letter, and slammed down the phone. My mind was racing. Should I call the police? Should I go outside and try to make some truce with Gene? Should I tell him my upstairs neighbor was the snitch and I'd beat her up for him if he wanted me to?

The next night when I left work, I got in my car and prayed for ten straight minutes. I haven't prayed that long since Catholic school. I promised God I wouldn't ask for anything else if he'd protect me from Gene.

When I rounded the corner to my street, Gene stared at me from the moment I hit the block. I looked up at him as I approached and nodded. As I put my key in the door, he said, "Let me ask you something. Did you call the SPCA on me?" As if on cue, the little pit bull ran out of the house and scampered up to me, his tail wagging. I shrank back from the pit bull like I was afraid of it, with just the tiniest hope that my badly acted fear of the dog would make Gene think I hated dogs and was the last person who would call the SPCA. It took everything I had to act disgusted by that puppy. I coo audibly whenever I see cute small things; dogs, babies, penises, it doesn't matter. It's just a natural reaction. The dog couldn't sense my fake fear and started licking my leg.

Gene walked over toward me and the puppy. I kept my eye on Gene in an "If you try anything dumb, I will kill you" fashion, knowing the only weapon I had on me was a rusted can of pepper spray I'd never tested. *Shit, I wish I knew where Gene bought his gun. Oh, I can't get one anyway because of my mental health record. Damn the law.*

Gene stood right in my face, his puppy nipping at my skirt. I held my keys in between my fingers, ready to puncture his eyeballs if he made one sudden move. We held each other's gaze for a second, then Gene reached down and scooped up his puppy. As he walked away, he called out to me. "My sister wants to have some words with you when she gets home."

I relaxed my grip on my keys and let myself in the front door. I got out of being shot by Gene, but dammit, I'm not fighting a thirteen-year-old girl. This is no way to live, I decided. I don't believe in what my ex's mother, the DC socialite said, but I know I'm not ready yet. I can't throw myself into the hood and change everything.

But I couldn't tell my mother all that. I just told her I needed a change. She didn't need to know I'd been a prisoner in my own home, never going out when I knew Gene's sister was outside. She didn't need to know that I moved to the hood and the only thing I (possibly) helped was a puppy.

"Well, if you're sure, I support you," my mother said. "Promise me you won't wear red or blue. Ever," she said, throwing my blue jeans into the Goodwill bin.

My Impossible Self

In American English, mulatto traces the distance
from a contaminant. In eighteenth-century Latin
America, mulatto was only one pinion on a carni-
val wheel. In the United States of the eighteenth
century, the condition of mulatto was an offense
when it was thought to issue from black male desire. When mulatto was the issue of white male
desire, mulatto was unspoken, invisible, impossible.

—*Richard Rodriguez*, Brown: The Last
Discovery of America

Two years to the day after I graduated from college, I be-
came a stripper and had to forget I was black.

First things first. Why would I strip? I just wanted to. It's one
item on my long list of things I wanted to do before I die. Get my
degree no matter how much debt I accumulate—done! Take my
outdoors-loving cat to the park on a leash and walk him like a dog
and not care how anyone stares at me—done! See if I had the
courage to strip in front of strangers—not done! I still had about a
month left before I moved to Los Angeles, so I would have to do it
someplace far, far away from Philly. Like Jersey. Or Delaware. I
didn't want some customer guy recognizing my curls while I was
at a goodbye dinner with my mother and thanking me for the lap
dance.

My stripper friend-of-a-friend, Morgan, suspected me of playing a prank on her when I called to inquire about an out-of-state place where I could dance.

Morgan shrieked. "Girl, when I started stripping you said it was because I have father issues! I *know* you're not stripping!"

"Morgan, that was back when I was young and judgmental. Okay, and I was jealous because I was two hundred pounds and *couldn't* strip. Not for money, anyway," I explained. "You know I live and let live now."

"Whew, then you having this desire to strip is some kinda serious karma for you, isn't it? Isn't it amazing how the universe presents lessons on being nonjudgmental? Anyway, we gotta get you some booty shorts and shit," Morgan said, in the same tone of voice one would use to mention they had to get some milk. "You can come with me and apply during my shift tonight. I'm in Delaware now. Tax laws are better down here and it's illegal to show full tit."

A couple of hours later, I was shopping on South Street with Morgan. It's a street best known for tattoo shops and hemp bracelet stores, where twentysomethings with blue hair walk next to teenage girls who look like they've just stepped out of a rap video. I'd been on this street numerous times; I'd been sneaking here since I was fifteen and told my mother I was going to the library. I thought I'd seen every square foot of every touristy trinket shop on the street, but with Morgan as my co-shopper, clerks led us into secret back rooms and upstairs areas away from the Philly Cheesesteak T-shirts and Liberty Bell alarm clocks. I felt like I was in one of those mansions I used to see on TV where rich people would press a button and an entire wall of books swiveled to reveal a safe.

These hidden rooms had stripper clothes with cutouts anyplace you wanted. There were also handmade originals for the more seasoned dancer. Is your favorite client too discriminating for your standard schoolgirl or nurse fantasy? He's always had a crush on Glenda the Good Witch? You're in luck, because her outfit is back here in thong style, complete with magic wand, which I assumed could be used to hit low-tipping patrons on the head.

After we visited three stores, Morgan took me to her favorite one. It had a pole in each dressing room so you could see if your outfit stretched enough for your routine. I could never play poker—my face gives away every thought going through my mind—so it didn't surprise me when a tired-looking blond girl with a mouth outlined in a lipliner three shades darker than her lipstick asked me if I was overwhelmed.

"First time? Well, if I could suggest something, I'd play up your exoticness."

If she was still reading my face, she'd know I was a little thrown off by her comment. I didn't think anyone would call me exotic in a clothing store *for* exotic dancers. White people love to say I look exotic. Black people like to dig around in my hair for answers to my ancestry ("I know you at least got a white grandmother hidden in those curls!"), but they will never come straight out and ask "What are you?" without the hair segue, and they damn sure don't call me exotic. Iman looks exotic. I look light-skinned and, perhaps, mixed.

White people, when in places where it's somewhat acceptable to comment on people's appearances (makeup counters, men buying you drinks in bars) usually go straight to "What are you?" or the aforementioned less-intrusive-sounding "You're so exotic!" followed by "Where are you from?" Sometimes I can't help but laugh out loud at how funny calling me exotic is. I grew up with dogs and took ballet lessons at the local YMCA. I had a crush on Ricky Schroder from *Silver Spoons* and, later, Cockroach from *The Cosby Show.* I got excited over spelling bees until I discovered boys. How much more American and unexotic can you get?

Whatever the race of the person asking questions about my background, I'm always embarrassed because it takes a normal situation (like shopping in exotic-dancer stores) and throws a spotlight on me. I like to choose when I make a spectacle of myself, thank you very much. Plus, though I try to hide it, it hurts especially when a black woman asks if I'm mixed. I always take it to mean that she doesn't see me as she sees herself, that I'm still not black enough, no matter how comfortable I feel checking off that box.

I feel an overwhelming need to prove myself to black women who question me, to tell them that no one on the white side of my family has called me since I was in the ninth grade. To explain that I love my mother and use her as the barometer of what I should be as I grow older: beautiful, strong, and black. "Girl, I don't even remember how to be half white!" I want to say. Occasionally, I want to give a smart-ass reply. "This is America, what color do you think I am?" Instead, I lie. To protect my feelings, I usually reply with a curt "I'm all black" in a tone that says, *This conversation is over.*

The blond shopgirl really wanted her sale and was convinced that commenting on my looks was the way to accomplish her goal. "Really," she continued. "You should play up that cultural thing. Where are you from?"

I had to answer the question in a way that would make her shut up and get on with the sale. I didn't need her telling me how her dad once had a Mexican mistress or have her feeling safe enough with my white side to whisper that she's always wanted to sleep with a black man (that's happened before—in a supermarket). I also wasn't sure if Morgan knew my dad is white, and I didn't want her to treat me differently right before escorting me into a house of dubious repute for the first time.

I took the safe route and responded as if I was dumb.

"I'm from here. Philly."

"No, originally. Where are your parents from?"

"Philly, too. I'm black. Where's your sales rack?"

After getting a bit mad at myself for letting her intrusion throw me off so much I rhymed that last sentence, I headed for the bargain booty-shorts section. Hell, I was a start-up stripper. I wasn't spending more than I had to.

I was digging through the discount bin and I started getting pissed that I couldn't buy a stripper outfit without potentially having to justify my self-identification and get into a discussion of how black is a set of shared experiences, not a complexion.

I wanted to get out of the store, so I grabbed the first matching sales things in my size. For $47.97, I scored pink Lucite platform heels, hot-pink boy shorts with matching bikini top, and a sheer white wrap skirt.

We were almost at Morgan's car when we walked by a wig store, and I realized I'd forgotten to buy a wig. We rushed in and I saw a long straight auburn wig. I interrupted two salesgirls comparing the airbrush designs on their nails to ask if they had the same wig in brown and, if so, could they just slap it tight on my head because I was going to wear it out.

The two young deep-brown-skinned black women looked up and twisted their faces into an incredible mix of disgust, surprise, and disbelief. They looked at me as if I'd just bounced into their wig store buck naked and yelled, "Pack your bags, girlies, you've won a trip to Fiji!"

The taller girl, with green lightning bolts on all her fingernails, asked, "Who is it for, you?"

Morgan and I were running a bit late, so there was no time to let these salesgirls try to convince me not to cover up all my good hair. No time for me to make my usual self-deprecating jokes about my hair not being as good as it looks. And no way to make them understand in a short amount of time that calling my hair *good* hurts me deeply. If they thought my hair was good, they thought my mother's hair was bad, and it had been that same pain of *bad* features that had caused her to think her mixed daughter would have it easier.

With Morgan looking at her watch, I put a little inflection in my voice that let the women know I was serious about the damn wig and they needed to get it now.

"Yes, it's for *me*. Can I try it on?"

"She's black," Morgan chimed in for no apparent reason. I'd have to tell her later that I usually only had to say that to nonblack people.

After learning that the Gwyneth was available only in auburn, paying the mandatory dollar wig-cap try-on fee, and having the salesgirl break into a sweat trying to stuff all my hair under the wig, Morgan told me it looked great and we had to go. With my auburn hair on, we headed to Delaware and a blinding neon Tattle-tales sign. Morgan damn near yanked my arm off as she rushed me through the strip club door, past the cavernous main club area, and into the dressing room. It looked like the typical backstage area of any fashion show, a couple of girls getting out of street clothes, wall-to-wall mirrors, lockers, a wide array of drugstore makeup scattered all over the vanity areas. The only visible differ-ence was the handwritten sign that said ANYONE CAUGHT GIVING EX-TRAS WILL BE FIRED! Then again, we had that sign when I worked at Roy Rogers.

Morgan instructed me to stay put while she talked to Alice the House Mom, a sixty-something chubby white woman with gray hair pulled into a schoolteacher bun. I had learned from my online research that the house mom takes care of all of the dancers' needs, from making a depressed girl smile to painstakingly apply-ing layers of concealer to a ten-inch tattoo of an ex-flame's name before a stripper hits the stage lights. Alice the House Mom looked like she should be judging the apple pie contest at the county fair instead of mothering strippers.

As Morgan talked to her, the dressing room door slammed open. A cute dark-haired girl rushed through the door, pissed. "Why do I sign up to work on Tuesday nights?" she whined. She snatched about twelve dollar bills from her G-string and stuffed them into her locker. I stared at her because she was about a size 14 with cellulite. I thought all the girls here would be perfect and would laugh when I auditioned. Seeing her curves gave me some relief, but I still couldn't believe I was going to have to audition almost naked in front of Alice the House Mom. I feel weird if my cats watch me undress. How would Alice judge me? I tried to breathe through my nervousness by doing an affirmation: I'm a badass. I can be in a spotlight and feel comfortable. I deserve better than hanging out on the edge and observing. I have a great butt.

Suddenly, Morgan pointed to me, and Alice the House Mom turned her head to check out the virgin stripper.

When we made eye contact, Alice's face relaxed a bit. Morgan started laughing.

"I was trying to tell you! She's not black! She's Puerto Rican, Asian, and . . . Irish," Morgan exclaimed, laughing.

Alice relaxed her shoulders and walked over to me. "Well, aren't you an exotic bitch," she said, smiling.

This was the first time I agreed with a white person about how exotic I am. The combination Morgan threw out there *was* exotic. I guessed, because my wig was almost red, that Morgan threw the Irish in there at the last second. Nice touch. I knew Alice the House Mom wasn't buying that mix, though. Was she that dumb?

"Is that your natural hair color?" Alice asked, in admiration of my synthetic locks.

Morgan, who was standing behind Alice, bugged her eyes out at me. I told Alice that it was a rinse. Wasn't that what white girls got? I didn't know.

"It's nice, bitch. You can audition tonight. Use locker four. Get changed."

Morgan grabbed me before I could unload my things into the locker. "I'm going to show her where the bathroom is."

As Morgan pulled me out the door, Alice yelled, "What size are her nipples? About a large?"

"Probably," Morgan yelled back.

I'd been in a strip club for five minutes, and so far I'd been stripped of my race and people were exchanging information about my nipples. This was too much! I noticed that I was sweating like a pig out of nervousness. I wanted to back out. I couldn't get up onstage in front of these men. What was I thinking? I hated my thighs!

I was thoroughly confused. Now that we were in the bathroom, out of Alice's earshot, I needed to ask Morgan what was going on and let her know I might bail out of this whole thing. "Morgan—"

"Shhhhh! You can't call me that in here. It's Coco. Coco Diamond. You gotta think of a name, too. You do not want these crazy guys knowing your damn real name. They'll be stalking you. They are all crazy. Take it from Coco Diamond."

Do all dancers name themselves according to their skin color? I had already heard the deejay announce a dancer named Butter Pecan. Dancers' names are kind of like porn stars' names, right? I remembered in high school your porn name was your pet's name followed by the street you grew up on. I was not too sure the guys would be turned on by the deejay announcing, "Welcome to the stage the beautiful, exotic Fatty Dicks!"

There can be only so many Dicks Avenues in America. What were the odds that my parents would choose that street to raise me on? Man, I missed our cat, Fatty, though. While I was contemplating my stage name, Morgan explained why she had to change my race.

"I didn't know Ebony was working tonight, or I wouldn't have had to tell Alice that you weren't black. They have a four-black-girls-a-night maximum. Just play it off. Shit, you look like you could be something else anyway, specially with that wig. You got any lotion?"

I always have lotion. What black girl doesn't carry lotion? There is nothing worse than having on shorts in junior high and a schoolyard full of boys pointing out that your knees are white and chalky while your body is brown. In the summer, I have regular lotion and lotion with SPF 30. I'm the only girl I know who can have ashy knees *and* sunburned shoulders.

While Morgan lotioned up, I threw cold water on my face and inquired again about my nipples.

"Alice meant your areola. I told you Delaware is real strict. She wanted to know what size tit cover to get you. We have to cover at least our areolas or they'll shut the club down," Morgan said. "There are more crazy rules, like, the dudes can't touch you at all and you can't touch dudes below the belt. You can stabilize yourself on their shoulders if you're giving them a private lap dance, but don't actually let your lap touch their lap. You'll get fired."

So, the guys would pay me *not* to touch me? Cool! Almost every time my girls and I go to a regular club, we have to pay to get in *and* some guys try to sneak a free feel while we're dancing.

One of Morgan's press-on nails popped off, so I decided that my stripper name would be Lee. I wanted something that could be a first or last name, Asian, Puerto Rican, or Irish. "Yes, Lee. Short for O'Reilly."

We left the bathroom in our street shirts and skimpy bottoms. Morgan introduced me to the deejay as Lee and asked if he could make sure we were on at the same time. When we got back in the dressing room, Alice held two little conical pieces against my shirt. They looked like two small Chinese farmer hats, except these had red sequins on them. Alice told me to try them on my breasts. When they fit, Alice told me to put some double-sided tape on them to make them stick; I owed her ten dollars for them, but I could pay her after I auditioned. She then gave me my locker key and told Morgan to take me on a tour until the deejay called my name. When my name was called, I was to report immediately to the stairs above the stage.

My audition would take place in front of the whole club? I thought I'd be spinning on some private pole while Alice graded my performance. I wanted to take off my hot-pink heels, throw my jeans back on, and thank Alice and Morgan for the experience, but my lifelong fear of being called a quitter was stronger than my fear of making a fool out of myself in front of horny men who paid women not to touch them.

On our way to the floor, Morgan reminded me to listen for my name. I told her she had to get me a shot of vodka or I was going to lose my confidence. She did and told me that if I unfolded my hands from my chest and smiled, I'd make more money. I told her that Puerto Asian Irish girls don't smile. I downed my Absolut, and my confidence went up. I'd been multiracial before; I could do this. I thought back to how my mother used to instruct me to tell people, "My dad is white and my mother is black." If I just told people that, she said, everything would be okay.

Just like David Hasselhoff being mixed, it was a lie. Instead of opening my mouth to educate people about my background, I learned to stand off to the side and study every new situation for signs of racial strife before going in. That didn't leave me many places to go. But here I was, in the corner of a strip club, using those same analytical skills to calm myself and make my environment feel secure.

I counted how many stairs I would have to descend to the stage when the deejay called my name. I estimated the square footage of the stage (about the size of an Olympic swimming pool) and counted how many neon lights zipped alongside it. I noticed how the soft red and blue spotlights shone down on the dancers and how the size 14 girl's cellulite was undetectable under the red and blue lighting. I made a note to get that lighting for my bedroom.

There were two poles onstage and always one girl on each pole. When a dancer heard her name, she descended the stairs and claimed the pole closer to the stairs. The previous pole dancer moved to the second pole, while the dancer who had just worked both poles walked around the stage bar to collect her tips.

Simple enough, but these dancers managed to be rhythmic, and they had on heels lower than mine. The vodka warming my chest wasn't enough to get me past the fear that Tattletales would transform into a comedy club when its patrons saw me in heels trying to keep the beat with whatever hard rock song the deejay played during my set (they didn't play rap or soul music; it was an upscale club). I wondered if everyone was insecure about how they looked while they were dancing or if it stemmed back to Fat Pam and her diagnosing my white half as the cause of most of my disabilities.

"You ain't nothing but a white girl. You better learn how to dance. Don't ever let anyone see you moving like that," she'd say.

I was too young to understand that my lack of rhythmic movement could be due to the contact high my little body was getting off her burning nickel bag. Now, even though I know I can dance, I still almost never get up at the beginning of a song or feel right when people gather around me and chant, "Go, Angie!" I think they really want my ass to leave.

* * *

The deejay had just called Coco Diamond to the stage, so I knew I was up next. Maybe if I fell off the pole, she'd find a way to make it look like it was planned. Maybe we could stage an erotic fake fight or something.

Morgan danced down the steps at the start of a George Michael song and swung around the pole with little more enthusiasm than people show when they are holding on to a pole inside of a bus. Three quarters through the song, the deejay called out, "Lee. Calling Lee to the stairs. Lee to the stairs." I climbed to the top of the stairs, gripping the handrails with my sweaty palms, and tried to breathe deep into my stomach as I felt my throat closing up.

I tried to calm myself by reminding myself of how strong I was and how part of living a good life was taking risks and making sure you didn't have a boring eulogy. I promised myself that I could say *no* to anything I was afraid of for at least six months after this without beating myself up for it. The deejay called out, "Let's welcome Lee to the stage!" and as I started walking down the stairs, I forced myself to make eye contact with the men looking up at me. Surprisingly, the nervousness vanished as I did this. The men were clapping and hooting and looking at me like I was the pop star they'd had hanging on their wall since they were fourteen. I was smiling and enjoying my power. I'd purposefully thrust myself into the spotlight with only a wrap, sequins, and a wig to cover me. It felt damn good.

I swirled around the pole, making eye contact with a man drinking alone, then bit my lower lip as if I was shy and looked away. I then quickly looked back and he looked embarrassed to receive so much attention from me. A Johnny Depp look-alike called out, "Wow, your breasts are real, aren't they?!" I swung around the pole again and nodded my head *yes* and gave him a smile of appreciation. I was still too nervous to let go of the pole or even attempt to climb up it, but I was still proud of how well I was doing.

The song wound down and the deejay asked the crowd to "Welcome Amber Lynn to the stage," so I strutted to the next pole and watched as a blond girl glided down the stairs and climbed up her pole in two seconds flat. Amber Lynn's movements screamed sex. She descended the pole, then flew up it again in time with the beat. How does she do that? Bitch probably had a tree house growing up. I suddenly felt incredibly unsexy.

Finally, the song faded out and the deejay told the men to give it up for it being my first time, and I scurried around the stage to collect any money the men weren't saving for Amber Lynn. Most of the guys slid at least a dollar into my G-string, and those who didn't tip gave me a sincere compliment about my breasts or quadriceps (who would have thought so many personal trainers go to strip clubs?). I felt a bit of the same high I get when I'm falling in love. I thanked them sincerely and wondered why I went to college.

I had to find out if I was hired. Alice said I did well for my first time and told me "Go make that money, bitch." As soon as I exited the dressing room, a white man in a suit approached me, told me he enjoyed my stage show, then asked where I was from.

"Philly."

"No, where originally?"

Oh, here we go again. But this time, I was not upset. Strip clubs are about fantasies, and my job was to be whatever this man wanted me to be. Suddenly my racial ambiguity wasn't something that caused me to retreat to the margins, hoping not to be noticed and questioned; it was a source of power. I tried to guess what this cheap-suited man wanted me to be. This man could have been an associate college professor, so I was afraid to say Asian, lest he'd just finished giving a lecture on East-West Relations Since 1800 or something.

"I'm Creole," I said, falling back on the lie I told during my freshman year of college.

"Creole, beautiful! I'm Mark. Talk in private?"

Wow, the first man I talked to asked me into the Champagne Room for a private dance! A private dance cost twenty dollars for ten minutes. Five dollars of that went to the house.

We entered a side room manned by a bouncer who collected the money from Mark. There were three girls in there already, not touching their Marks. The bouncer sternly told my Mark the rules: Ten minutes and it's over. You want more? You pay. Keep your hands where I can see them. Enjoy yourself, brother.

How could a man enjoy himself when he'd just been barked at like he'd sped through a school zone? *Keep your hands where I can see them?* I was embarrassed for Mark. Weirdly, Mark didn't seem to care. I led him to a couch and told him to sit down. He listened better than kids I've babysat for.

I tried to watch what the other girls were doing while Mark broke the silence by telling me how he spent fifty out of fifty-two weeks on the road and had top-tier status on two airlines. I danced for Mark and I hoped the look on my face didn't betray my boredom while he ran down the benefits of being a Premier Executive 1K member at United Airlines. His time was up; he thanked me for the dance and asked if I'd have a drink with him out on the floor later. I smiled and said, "If some other man doesn't snatch me up first."

That's the boldest thing I've ever said to a man in a club. I get self-conscious when guys in nightclubs only dance two dances with me and then lean in and say thank you. When they do that, I run and check my nose for boogers, and if there's nothing in there I'm all, *Why doesn't he like me?*

And hell, Mark was white; there was a time I couldn't even speak to white men; they terrified me. It took me eight years of therapy to figure out that my fear had a connection to anger I felt toward my father. Thank God for therapy. If there is one thing that will guarantee failure in America, it's white-man-phobia.

I wished my college therapist were there to see that I'd just looked a grown white man in the eye and told him I couldn't guarantee I'd be available to have a drink with him. My more-evolved brain always knew it didn't make any sense to fear conversation with all white men, just like it didn't make sense to take the long way to work to avoid the corner where I had my first car accident.

So far, my first private dance had done more than talk therapy. Could I take and use this boldness in real life or did it only work in soft lights when I was wearing a wig? Did it only work when I was not black? Any other time, I was fighting to be black, but here I felt no shame about being everything but. Now, if I'd won a Nobel Prize and the selection committee told me they had a four-black-recipient limit and I'd have to say I was Irish and Asian to get my Peace Prize, I'd be pissed—but I was a stripper. Did the world really need one more black stripper? Who was I hurting by claiming *other* for one evening?

To fulfill customers' fantasies, other dancers had to hustle backstage to change outfits; I simply had to change nationalities and I could do that while wearing the same bargain getup, thanks to my mixed-race heritage.

The next four hours were just as easy and filled with more Marks. I smiled at men; they told me about their jobs, and I acted like fixing copiers/day trading/being the-guy-at-the-car-wash-who-drives-the-wet-cars-over-to-be-dried was the most exciting and sexually stimulating thing I'd ever heard. With only a few minutes left in my shift, I looked for Morgan. Stripping was so easy, I was thinking about coming back again. So far tonight I'd been Russian, Sicilian, Papua New Guinean, Mexican, and Jewish. I even got real bold and told one drunk guy with Argyle socks that I was Argylean.

On my way to see if Morgan was in the dressing room, a group of young men in business suits called me over to their table. As I approached, the alpha male of the group shouted, "We need you to give our friend Mike a private dance. Help us loosen him up!"

I smiled at Mike, who was looking down and waving his hands in front of his face to protest all the attention. Mike looked like he hoped the chair would suck him up and spit him out anywhere but here. I grabbed his hand and promised him that a dance would be fun. Mike wouldn't budge from the chair.

Alpha Male said, "I think he needs more than a dance. He needs your big ass in his face." He then lapsed into the best slave accent he could muster. "Hoo-hoo, honey chile, how did you get such a black ass? How much to buy that?"

I would rather he had spit on me and punched me in the stomach. I was speechless.

Was he drunk? Was my face showing how much that comment and accent had hurt me? My entire shift, I'd freed myself; I'd allowed myself to shed all the protective layers I carry, but it seems I also forgot why I carry them. Because I'm intensely vulnerable when it comes to being judged on any aspect of my blackness, I have myriad ways to deal with every question about my identity. It's why I cut my hair short, so no one could call it good, why I still sneak to the tanning salon with another half-white girl so we can get our complexions to that perfect warm brown level where no one asks us, "Are y'all mixed?" This drunk strip-club-going fuck had just stripped me of my four-hour high. And all I could do was remain silent and smile.

I realized I was half naked with dirty dollar bills sticking out of my shorts, and suddenly it was hard to feel powerful. *Honey chile?* Was he trying to be funny or cool? Could I tell a customer, *Fuck you?* I knew I could if he tried to manhandle me, but what he'd just done hurt more than that.

I think I said something cutesy about not wanting to take their money when they were so obviously drunk, but I know I ran back to the dressing room to find Morgan. It was definitely time to go home. Since it was change of shift, the room was a maze of girls and sequins and concealer. I spotted Morgan taking out her colored contacts in the far mirror. I rushed over and started telling her about the slave accent and the honey-chile comment.

"Please," Morgan said, dismissing my complaint while she blinked out one of her faux green eyes. "You just have to get used to that. The guys in here think they own you; they get a little liquor and grow some chest hair. Just walk away."

I wasn't ready to tell her I was done with this place and she was the proud owner of my hot-pink heels if she wanted them. If I ever experienced a high and crash like that again, it would have to be from something illegal.

As I cringed at the pain of taking the tape off the most sensitive area of my breasts, Amber Lynn threw the dressing room door open and hobbled over to Alice.

"All you black bitches better open your lockers right now!"

For once in my life, my brain was ahead of my mouth, so I knew not to object to the term *black bitches*. I had promised Morgan I wouldn't be black; I didn't want to get her in trouble. This was her daily job. Besides, "bitch" was mostly a term of endearment in that dressing room.

All the black-identifying women turned toward their lockers without more than a few *here we go again* mumbles. Alice put ice in a condom and applied it to Amber Lynn's ankle while addressing the black dancers.

"This is the second fall one of y'all has caused this week." As soon as each of the black girl's lockers was open, Alice the House Mom rummaged through her belongings, seemingly disgusted that she couldn't find what she was looking for.

"I'm going to say it one last time: no lotion anywhere on your bodies if you're going to use the poles. I don't want to hear any complaints about being ashy or whatever you call it. Slippery poles break bones. Lotion and poles are a deadly combination. Is that understood?"

I tried to suppress a giggle while Amber Lynn got up and tried to walk off her ankle pain.

Morgan motioned for me to head toward the bathroom with her. I grabbed my pocketbook with the big bottle of Keri lotion in it and followed her. I couldn't believe they hadn't searched my locker. I wished they had posted a NO LOTION sign; I hadn't meant to hurt anyone. That place needed an employee handbook.

As soon as we got in the bathroom, I burst out laughing. *Lotion and poles are a deadly combination!* It sounded like an antimasturbation lecture they'd given the boys at my Catholic elementary school.

Morgan joined in my laughter. "Girl, that is hardly the reason why those white girls fall. Those girls are uncoordinated." Morgan rattled on. "Amber shouldn't try to slide backward down a pole when she's drunk. I can't make money with ashy knees. I knew they only inspect black girls' lockers, and once we said you weren't black, they wouldn't look at yours. I'm-a need you to carry the lotion every night."

"Girl, you're stronger than me if you can put up with this every night."

Morgan stopped laughing and started into her usual speech about numbing herself and just playing along with whatever people want you to be.

She didn't know I struggled not to do that every damn day. And I hated it. I couldn't willingly let people define me again, especially if it meant not being black. I just hoped to draw on some of the boldness I had gained there and use it more often in my daily life. My armor was getting heavy.

Besides, I had more important things on my to do list, and now that I'd found out I could fool people just by wearing a wig, I wanted to think of a few more things to add to that list. Maybe I could infiltrate other cultures and see what they said when they thought no black people were around.

The idea excited me. I turned to walk to the bathroom door and noticed that my elbows were ashy. Damn, I got ashy quick. Until I found the perfect lotion, I'd have to limit myself to cultures that got ashy like black people. I lotioned my elbows up and straightened my wig. Hiding the Keri deep in my pocketbook again, I teetered on my stilettos and followed Morgan to say goodbye to my fellow strippers.

Fat, Black, and Ugly

Although the bitterness that some black women feel over intermarriage is well known, the imbalance rests even more heavily on Asian-American men. For every 1,000 Asian women with husbands, only 860 Asian men had wives, leaving a large number of Asian bachelors left over. In contrast, for every 1,000 black women who were married, there were 1,059 black married men.

—*"2000 Census Shows Interracial Marriage Gender Gaps Remain Large," UPI, March 14, 2003*

Are you half black and half white? Feeling unattractive? Before you revert to plastic surgery, consider a simple change of venue. You'll find you can go from ugly to amazing in one day, with no anesthesia or scarring!

Take this example: A is a twenty-six-year-old mixed girl. She's average height, with a healthy weight according to government guidelines.

She goes to a predominantly white Center City Philadelphia bar. She's a bit too plump and too dark for the men. She sits all night and watches thinner white girls get hit on.

She gives up and goes to a bar down the street where the majority of patrons are black—and suddenly she's stunning! She gets complimented on the extra meat on her ass and watches as bigger, darker women get ignored.

Maybe being pretty isn't enough for you? Perhaps you'd like to lose all traces of your black side? Again, before you go all Vin Diesel on us, try a quick trip out of the United States.

Same mixed girl, same size, in Rio de Janeiro: Fat but white. *Brazil has an entirely different racial classification system!* "There is no one-drop rule here! No one judges you on the ethnicity of your parents," A's tour guide told her. "Here, it's all about how light your skin is and how much money you have." As A was staying in a four-star hotel with an all-white American tour group, she too enjoyed the privilege of being white for five days!

Whatever you do, mixed girl of average weight; be very careful if you choose to move to Hollywood. When A went there, she found she was considered unattractive by men of every race. She sat in bars and watched as white and black men both flocked to women blonder and thinner than she was.

According to the 2000 census, 4.9 percent of people in Los Angeles County consider themselves mixed-race. That's more than twice the national average. I'd love to find out how all those mixed-race couples met; I saw only white people my first month in Los Angeles. "Where are the black people?" I finally asked the first black person I met, the guy who delivered my sofa.

"Magic Johnson's Friday's," he answered. He was right. I drove by there one night and, like magic, all the white people disappeared a few blocks north of the restaurant.

Still, gas was too expensive and traffic too brutal to drive to Friday's every night. How does anyone, let alone interracial couples, get together in LA? I wondered. Los Angeles is so spread out, no one walks; everyone lives in their own bubble inside their air-conditioned car. I was lonely. I called the one person I knew who had lived in Los Angeles. Davina was a black writer who gave up on Los Angeles after three years, not because she couldn't find a job but because she couldn't find a man. I broke down to Davina over the phone. "I hate this city. I hate the segregation, I hate the smog, and is it me or does every black man in this city look right through me?"

Davina laughed like she'd heard the frustrated ramblings of black female LA transplants numerous times before. "Girl, back east, the black men want black women who look close to white. In LA, they done went all the way; they only date white. Trust me, they'll make babies who look like you, but they won't date you."

"What do I do for dates? For sex? For someone to put together my coffee table?" I asked her.

"Go find an Asian man," she said. "They're going through the same thing as us. When's the last time you seen an Asian woman with an Asian man?"

I honestly couldn't remember.

After almost a year of celibacy and unrequited flirting with Toshi, my Japanese neighbor, I decided to divert my attention from my lack of dates by surrounding myself with female friends. I put an ad up on the clubs section of Craigslist: "African American Book Club Forming." Eight black women responded. We talked about books for one meeting; after that, we gave up even acting like we were reading.

"I wish I had a man. If I did, y'all would never see me again," Leslie, a beautiful struggling actress, said.

"Well, I guess we'll be seeing a lot of you. This is Hollywood. If you see a brother with a sister, it's his biological sister," someone responded. I had recently started working for a production company. Of the six black guys there, five had white wives and one was dating an Asian girl. Whenever I'd walk on the studio lot and see a black man with a black woman, I'd smile and stare longingly. *Wow, there is still hope.*

"Give it up," Janine, a stunning woman with legs up to her neck and a sexy European accent, said, making a dismissive motion with her hand. "I'm forty, and I haven't found one yet. If you want to stay in California, you deal with it."

Most of us met Janine's lecture with teeth-sucking; we refused to give up the fight even though it was clear we weren't winning.

"I'm telling you, y'all should start dating white guys," said

Nikki, a thirty-year-old kindergarten teacher who was usually quiet throughout the meetings. "I've just started, and let me tell you—they know how to treat a woman." She smiled coyly.

"You must be lying," I said. "I've been in clubs, and not one white man would give me the time of day."

"Girl, every race of people in LA bars is crazy. You've got to go online," she whispered, as if telling me where buried treasure was hidden.

White men? No way, I can't do it. First of all, I knew they didn't all treat their women well. I'd had too many visits to child support court as a kid to think that. Second, I'd made a promise to my mother when she was in the fifth year of trying to divorce my father that I'd never marry a white man.

"Can you believe the judge had the nerve to ask your father if he was sure you were his children?" my mother asked me, exhausted from another day at court. "I'm telling you, love may be blind, but the justice system isn't—especially when you're a black woman trying to leave a white man."

I imagined my mother's face and her thoughts if she saw me return home from LA with a white guy: *Dear Jesus, didn't she learn anything from what I went through?*

Still, it wasn't like I hadn't disobeyed my mother in the past. I decided to upload my best photo to Match.com. I'll just try a little bit of white, I thought, as if I were on a diet and the Caucasian race were a piece of cheesecake.

After I uploaded my photo, I checked off that I was looking for men of all races within a hundred-mile area. But that sounded pretty desperate, so I limited the distance range to fifty miles and took Latinos off my wanted list. Then I wondered if that seemed racist, so I took Native American men off, too.

The initial plan was to ease my way into dating white men by starting with Jewish guys. They're not *really* white, I reasoned. No Jewish guys responded to my ad. I later found out that most of the mensch daters hung out at Jdate.com. God knows I wasn't about to put a photo of my black self up over there.

After automatically deleting all e-mails from white men, I started corresponding with Andrew. After a couple of e-mails, I had learned he was from Connecticut and that his parents were both Protestant doctors who paid his way through Northwestern so he wouldn't be burdened with working and studying at the same time.

Lord, how much more white can he get? I thought. *Well, if you're going to learn how to swim, might as well jump in the deep end.*

In his e-mails, Andrew never told me what he did for a living; I'd asked him three times, but he seemed always to skip right over that question. *Cool, I like a bit of a challenge, but he better not be unemployed.*

I was intrigued about why Andrew had e-mailed me. What in my profile suggested to him that we'd be a match? Maybe he has a black-girl fetish? I'll bet he has some pretty, thin blond fiancée waiting in the wings and he's using me to fulfill his interracial fling fantasies before he weds Becky.

When Andrew hadn't responded to my last e-mail in three days, I convinced myself that there *was* a Becky and that Andrew was a horrible racist, despite all evidence to the contrary. Just before I typed a "have a happy marriage, white supremacist!" e-mail, I saw a new message from him. He finally admitted to his job. He was a movie stuntman and had been on set twelve hours a day for the past three days, hence the late reply.

Lord knows my dating history suggests I love dangerous men, especially dangerous men with a high possibility of being brain damaged, so I e-mailed him right back and asked if his parents were pissed that they spent Northwestern tuition on a son who jumped out of moving vehicles and got shot with rubber bullets.

The next day Andrew instant-messaged me and said his dad had been upset for years but was now over it. We ended up talking on the phone that night, and the most exciting part for me was finding out that his voice was deep and not nasal like the white anal-retentive stereotypical voice I expected.

Andrew spoke slowly and put thoughtful pauses in his speech when I asked him questions. I love that. Nothing like a good pause instead of a drawn-out "uhhhhh." If he was black, I'd have been thinking, *Omigod, hecouldbetheone,* but instead I thought, *He could still be a serial killer who hears voices telling him to kill medium-sized black girls.*

Despite my reservations, I accepted his offer to meet him for sushi on Third Street in Santa Monica the next night. I'll start cutting carbs next week, I thought.

Third Street Promenade is the closest thing you'll find to Times Square in Los Angeles. The stores stay open late; there are crowds of different-colored people walking around checking out street performers and getting their caricatures drawn by Asian men. (So this is where the rest of them are. If it doesn't work out with Andrew, I'll come back here.)

Because of the crowds, it's the perfect place to meet an Internet date—you can easily happen to "get lost" if the person looks nothing like their photo. Since Andrew had revealed he was a stunt actor, I was a little concerned that he would arrive on a mobility scooter powered by a breathing tube and ask if I minded pushing him around all night.

Thankfully, I didn't need to hide. Andrew was waiting for me in front of the sushi spot, and he looked just like his photo. About five foot eleven, thick curly hair, green-gray eyes, and a nice olive complexion. He was darker than I am. Usually I think it's a bit unfair when white people have a deeper complexion, but on Andrew it looked perfect.

He greeted me with what felt like a reluctant hug. Oh, God, I thought, is he being reluctant because he thinks I'm ugly or is he feeling as weird as I am because we've talked but never met?

Andrew had called ahead for reservations, so we sat down right away. Since he was also from the other side of the country, we did what most transplanted East Coasters do enthusiastically when making small talk: make an exhaustive list of things that are so much better about the East Coast, then realize we sound like whiners and wind the conversation down with "But, boy, you can't beat the weather out here."

Once we finished small-talking about being blessed with the ability to go "to the beach and the mountains all in the same day," we talked about his job.

Andrew pulled up his sweater sleeve to show me a thick, jagged scar that ran the length of his forearm.

"Would you believe I got that from an independent movie?" Andrew said.

Yup, I could sleep with this man, I thought, as the waitress put the California rolls down on our table. He's definitely tough enough not to back down from any brothers who might have a problem that I'm dating him. Being able to scare off a militant brother was a requirement for any white man I dated. I knew at least one angry black man would purposefully bump into him or call me a sellout under his breath when I walked hand in hand with Andrew. I'd heard my mother's stories about dating my father. Then again, this is LA. You can go months without seeing black people.

Of course, I wasn't sure if Andrew liked me. I mean, I'm pretty confident with black men, but I couldn't shake the idea that white men prefer leggy blondes. That's the type of girl who is always on their magazine covers, right? Why would a fine white guy with a degree and a job want to date a black woman?

My "I must be the representative for all black people" paranoia started to kick in as well. I couldn't just have a one-night stand with him even if I wanted to; he might think all black women are easy. When our main dishes came, I hoped I wouldn't forget how to use chopsticks or get a piece of rice in between my teeth. Andrew would probably go to work the next day telling everyone, "Well, that's the last black girl I date. That's a race of messy eaters, right there." Even on dates, I had to be a credit to my race. Damn, it's a heavy burden, feeling like you're always under a microscope. Somewhat like a celebrity, I suppose. If black people can't get reparations, we should at least get free goody bags and commercial endorsements for this burden. Shit.

Andrew seemed to be enjoying my company and the food, so I tried to quiet my neuroticism. I made it through the sushi without incident and after he paid the bill (and left the appropriate tip— yes!), he suggested we take a walk. That he didn't want to end the date right away was a positive sign that loosened me up a bit. Forget about his race and just act how you would act with a black guy, I told myself. If Andrew was going to like me, he was going to have to like regular ol' black me.

We got up and walked down the promenade past a toy store window. I pulled him inside the store. In the front was a hand puppet display. Andrew grabbed a firefighter puppet and put his hand inside it.

"I want a puppet!" I said.

"I only talk puppet," Andrew replied through the firefighter. "You have to talk to me through a puppet."

I was feeling a bit self-conscious. I'm not one to just pick up a rag doll and talk in a cartoon-character voice on a first date, but what the hell. I promised to stop worrying about what people think. I noticed one black puppet on the rack and decided I would talk back to him with the African American doll.

My hand snapped back when I noticed the black girl puppet had on a gold chain, gold earrings, tennis sneakers, and a T-shirt that said BASKETBALL IS MY LIFE. Hell, no, I thought. I am not talking with Stereotype Doll. I twirled the puppet rack around to find another black doll. Could I get a firefighter like Andrew? A cop, a doctor—hell, a waitress, even?

There were two other black puppets among the white ones on the display. Both were males, both had on two gold hoop earrings, sneakers, jeans, gold chains, and logo shirts. One had on a do-rag. Why, God, why?

Andrew still had his white firefighter puppet on his hand, with a look on his face like, Are you going to choose a doll, or am I going to stand here looking like an idiot?

"Who made that puppet?" I asked Andrew. He looked at the tag. "Sunny Puppets," he said, his face suggesting asking for the name of a toy manufacturer was a weird inquiry.

"Well, fuck Sunny Puppets," I said, trying as hard as possible to laugh and keep the mood light. That's what I would have said with a black man, so I said it to Andrew. *Keepin' it real, what?*

Andrew, looking a little confused, lowered his fireman. I didn't mean to scare him with my shift in attitude, but how could I explain to a white guy how much seeing a rack with only gold-chain-and-sneakers-wearing black puppets pissed me off? Would he understand? If he didn't, I wasn't ready to hear it yet. Andrew might be a really nice guy, he'd just never had to deal with his people being portrayed as puppets without jobs. He never had to ask if there was a firefighter puppet in the back that looked like him. Toys that looked like him were always on display.

Still, I didn't want this date to go south. Freakin' smiling gold-chain puppets. There was a white cop puppet. A white doctor puppet. A white army puppet. Why couldn't there be at least one black military puppet for me to pick up? There are black people in the military! The top U.S. military commander was black! Where is the damn Colin Powell puppet?

I had to get away from the puppet rack. Toy stores are supposed to be fun.

"I have a new game," I said, leading Andrew away from the display with his nonpuppeted hand. "It's called Find the Black Doll Not Wearing a Gold Chain."

Andrew looked like he wanted to laugh but wasn't sure if he was allowed to. I smiled to let him know it was okay. We started our game in the first aisle, with me leading the way.

"Ooh! Black girl doll! Six o'clock!" I picked up a Barbie-type box with the word FLAVAZ emblazoned across the front. According to the box, the doll's name was Kiyoni Brown. Kiyoni came complete with boom box and tight pants (maybe I can forgive that;

Barbie dresses like a ho sometimes). But I couldn't forgive Kiyoni's gold chain, which meant the game was not over. We had to keep looking!

Andrew started getting into it. He pointed to a wall of Matrix dolls. "Look! Laurence Fishburne! Morpheus doesn't have on a gold chain!" Andrew was right, but c'mon, Laurence Fishburne couldn't count. He's a black man in real life and of course I've never seen him wear a gold chain. Though I'd bet money that if they come out with a line of Fishburne dolls, someone in marketing will try to stick a chain on at least one of them. No points for the Fishburne doll.

"They have to be fictional dolls," I protested. "Not based on movies or real people."

Andrew looked sad, or maybe he was tired of the game. I didn't know. Hey, I said I was going to act the same way I would act if I were out with a black man, and this was definitely a game I would play with a brother. It's a variation of the very popular African American game Find the Black Person. It's mostly played at opera houses, exclusive restaurants (busboys don't count), watching Nascar races on television, and when you move into a new suburban neighborhood, but you're allowed to tweak the game any way you want. Black people are innovative like that.

Andrew and I continued the game to the other side of the store. "Let's split up," I suggested. "We'll find one faster that way." I headed toward the toddler toy section, leaving Andrew facing a shelf of ceramic dolls. "They're all white except for Pinocchio!" he cried. I had already moved on.

I was in the toddler section when I heard him yell out again. "I found one!" I started to walk over to him, but seconds later he called out, "Never mind. Nonfiction doll. It's a Diana Ross Barbie by Bob Mackie."

Determined not to leave the store until I had found a nice normal black doll, I headed to the back, where the breakable dolls are kept in glass cases under lock and key.

Finally. Three beautiful black dolls chilling in designer gowns surrounded by their white and Latina friends. I couldn't touch them because the display was locked, but, like visiting my ex–high school boyfriend in jail, it was comforting just seeing them behind the glass. God bless this dollmaker, I sighed. Everyone is getting Madame Alexander dolls for presents this year.

I walked over to Andrew. "I won," I told him proudly. After I proved it to him by walking him back to the Madame Alexander dolls, we walked back outside and watched a group of Mexican kids break-dance as a crowd formed a circle around them. "C'mon, white people, you can move closer," the leader of the dancers urged. "We're not in a gang!" I didn't laugh. Andrew laughed loudly along with the rest of the white people.

As the stores were shutting down, Andrew walked me back to my car. He had hung in there through my game; he hadn't made a mad dash out of the toy store once we split up on our non-gold chain-wearing black doll search. I really could like this guy, I thought. I don't think he thought the same; he nearly shoved me in my car before giving me a cheerful wave and jogging off. "I'll call you!" he yelled, from across the parking lot.

As I drove home, I pictured Andrew at work, suiting up for his fall off a bridge and telling people about the psycho black chick he went on a date with. "Then she told me the Fishburne doll didn't count."

Still, I felt proud of myself. At least I had tried to date a white man. But I wasn't going to end up in a relationship with him, so I hadn't betrayed my mother! Her struggle was not in vain, I thought. I called her and told her about my date, awaiting her supportive cheers and motherly reassurances that I was smart and beautiful and that one day the perfect black man would come for me on a white horse or in his pearl SUV. Instead, I heard thirty seconds of silence followed by a long exhalation.

"Angela, why would you put that poor white boy through all that?"

Huh? "Mom, I thought you'd be supportive. Remember when I was eleven and you told me not to marry a white man?"

"Girl, I was just mad at the system. Don't miss out on a good man because of something I said over fifteen years ago! Just find someone who loves you. I want some grandbabies before I die." She yawned. "I'm going to bed." She hung up.

All the worry I had that I would let her down by dating a white guy, and she got mad and hung up on me? Damn, why didn't she give me that white-guy-dating permission when I first moved out here? It would have been more useful than the Target gift certificate.

Before I went to bed, I logged on to my account and expanded my search to include all races. Then, in a purely selfish move, I checked off every box possible for my race when the system prompted me so I'd get tons of matches and make up for all that lost time.

White Thug, Black Panther Part II

"Your mom knew I was white," my father said, laughing. "I mean, come on, I have red hair and green eyes." He said this as if I might have forgotten, since I hadn't seen him in over twenty years.

I thought it only fair to get my father's side of the story. Like the judge always used to do when he was in child-support court. I had talked myself out of calling him for months. How do you start interviewing your father when you know your mailman better than you know him? What small talk would I use to start the conversation? *Hey, Dad! Remember that day the police had to escort Mom into your house to get the rest of my clothes? Good times, huh?*

The conversation went more smoothly than I anticipated. My father's mouth was on waterfall mode, asking questions of himself and then answering them. Of course, a lot of them had nothing to do with his marriage to my mother.

"Did I ever tell you about the scathing letter to the editor I wrote about the gas rate hike?" my dad asked, laughing again. "I know that's why they turned off my gas."

"What about the dancing date where Mom asked if you were white?" my brother asked. Thank goodness for his interjection. I made my brother make the call with me, since he and my father spent a lot of time together, especially since Jack III was born. My brother was barely four when my mom left my dad, so unlike me, he doesn't have all the bad preseparation memories. Mom reintroduced them when my brother was seven. My brother and my dad would go on trips while I stayed home and imagined Dad didn't exist. When people would ask me how I got so light when my mom has a deep brown complexion, I'd lie. "My dad is light-skinned," I'd say, reasoning in my mind that my dad does indeed have light skin, so it wasn't really lying.

"I can't dance! There never was a dancing date!" my dad said. "I did take her to an oldies night, but it was a sit-down date with theater-style seating."

"Great date," I said. I couldn't imagine a worse date than being stuck in a hardback chair listening to oldies. I'm surprised my mom gave him a second chance after that one.

My father started defending the merits of a sit-down musical date ("You see, the point is to talk while the music is playing. . . ."). This caused my brother to laugh through his nose, his snorts drowning out my father's words.

"You can't dance! You're so white! Sit-down oldies night! Bwa-hahahah!" my brother screamed and snorted. I heard Jack III crying in the background. "Hold on, I have to give my son his medicine. Wooooo." My brother's phone dropped to the floor. I heard his whooping cease as he calmed his son.

"Couldn't Mom have thought you were black because she thought your black stepdad was your biological dad?" I asked.

"My stepdad died before I even met your mom," Dad answered, as if he was dumbfounded that Mom would say that. "Unless she thought Mr. Earl, our landlord, was my stepdad. But that man was old enough to be my mom's grandfather." I wondered why my dad called his landlord Mr. Earl. I had never heard a white person address people with "Mr." in front of their first name. Maybe he was blacker than he thought.

My brother picked the phone back up, still laughing. "My boy loves his medicine. It tastes like bubble gum and raspberries," he explained. "I like it, too." I imagined my 250-pound brother with his thick Philly-boy beard and saggy pants sneaking a taste of his son's berry-flavored medicine. My mind wandered to all the times people raced to cross the street when they saw him coming. My brother's ethnicity rarely gets questioned. His son's will. My brother carried on the biracial tradition and married a woman with a black father and a white mother. Their son has gray eyes and hair that doesn't snag even if you run a fine-tooth comb through it.

I asked my father about the men who confronted him when my mom and he were on dates. He paused, trying to remember any, but came up blank. I wondered if my mom was more sensitive to them because she's black or if my father didn't want to admit in his first conversation with his estranged daughter that he used to whup people's asses for looking at him sideways.

"I don't remember any serious problems. I remember this white guy in Sears staring at us. We were on the up escalator and he was on the other one, going down. He kept staring at us, so I said, 'Why don't you take a photo? It will last longer.'" My dad laughed.

My brother asked, "What was it like being white around mostly black people?"

"I didn't think much of it. I grew up around all white people, then the neighborhood started changing. When we moved to 56th Street, I was one of the only white people around, but I didn't think much of it. Back then, I had jobs where there were only white people around, but I didn't see anything weird about that either. That's just the way my mom raised me."

Of course you didn't notice anything wrong with the store having only white employees, I wanted to say. *You're white.* A black person would notice, especially if he tried to put in a job application. I didn't say anything because I wasn't sure what I expected from him. From what my mom said, I thought he was so black he almost didn't know he was white. Oh, well, hopefully I still have some ass-whupping stories coming up.

"I met your mom while I was playing chess with her sister, Bea.

She was the only one on the block who could play chess," my dad said, toppling his status in my mind from a Fonzie-like thug dad to a Sears-shopping, chess-playing dad who gets his comebacks from *MAD* magazine cartoons. *Take a picture, it will last longer?* Who says that when they're grown?

"But I remember you play-fighting with friends on the street!" I exclaimed, leaving my brother and father to figure out how I made the leap from chess to play-fighting.

"We'd do that just to get a rise out of people," my dad replied.

"I do that, too!" my brother yelled, like a little boy happy that he had something in common with his father. "If I'm following behind my friend in a car and we both come to a red light, we'll jump out and start fighting in the street for ten seconds, then jump back in our cars and drive off."

I made a mental note to tell my brother not to do that. Didn't he know a black man jumping out of his car play-fighting was different from a white guy doing it? I thought back to when my mom lamented that she let my brother visit my dad. "Can a white man raise a black child?" she asked her hairdresser, Miss Lillian. "Yeah, if you want your son to get shot," she answered.

"Dad, have you ever been in a real fight?" I asked, clinging to the hope that he had a little tough guy in him. I've got a soft spot for those guys. The Al Pacinos, the Indiana Joneses, the cute little rappers who wear Band-Aids over their bullet scars.

"Yeah, I got into a fight in high school. It lasted three punches. This guy Bill punched me in the nose, but it started bleeding, so he went to the corner store to get some tissues for me. We became best friends after that."

Okay, white thug has totally left the building. I asked him something I had always been curious about, since all the mistresses I remembered were black.

"Have you ever dated a white woman?"

Another pause. "Once. No, twice."

I never understood when people say they don't see color but only date people of a certain race. I tried not to judge, because, hey, that preference resulted in me being on earth, but I didn't understand.

"Why does anyone prefer anything? It's just what you prefer. Why do some people prefer chocolate ice cream over vanilla? I prefer black women."

"I hear that!" my brother screamed. The conversation had left me a little drained, and I wasn't sure if my brother was screaming for ice cream, black women, or black women who prefer ice cream.

I told my father I'd call him later, though I wasn't sure if I would. I was confused. I just wanted the story of how he met my mother; I thought perhaps I would glean some insights about race and love. How two people find each other in the middle of the melting pot. What he told me totally contradicted the story my mother gave me.

While I was trying to make sense of it all, I suddenly wondered if their relationship wasn't the perfect metaphor for how people feel when they're trying to figure out what I am. Everyone sees the same thing, but they each have different interpretations about how it all came together.

The Bright Girl in the Photo

"I yam what I yam and that's all what I yam."

—*Popeye the Sailor,*
on individualism

The day before my mother's wedding to Reverend Rob, I was lying in my backyard, trying to get a tan.

"Angela, we have a lot to do," my husband said. "Shouldn't you start packing?"

Getting a bit of sun was more important than packing. Whenever I take photos with my mother, I am struck by the difference in our complexions. The flash makes my skin turn bright white, while hers lights up to a color that reminds me of a nice warm cup of hot chocolate. I always imagine people seeing the photos and thinking, Who invited the ghost? Or that they would make the perfect promo poster for the updated version of *Imitation of Life*.

I explained this to my husband. He acted like he got it, but even I understood that this much obsession with getting browner for my mother's wedding photos was a bit abnormal.

Maybe I'm trying to burn away the guilt, I thought, only a bit facetiously. I feel like I put my mother through a lot, growing up. I thought about the time I shouted, "I hate black people!" after giving her Fat Pam's weed leftovers. How, when I got older, I apologized for it and she brushed the apology away. "You were only twelve; you were going through an identity crisis," she said. "I know how that is. I used to get teased so bad for being dark-skinned, I used to sleep with clothespins on my nose and tried to bleach my skin."

That made me feel even worse. I wondered if Jacqui or Maureen did the same thing after I teased them or ignored them because of their darker skin. I felt bad because I'd had plenty of opportunities to heal my racial emotional scars. I wondered if Maureen and Jacqui had had a chance to do the same. Did they believe me when I looked down on them? Were Jacqui and Maureen buying bleaching creams and clothespins today?

I thought of how, a few weeks before, I overheard a group of junior high students I tutored call a classmate "black and burnt." How I tried in my calmest voice to explain that black people separating each other by color was a horrible hurtful thing we learned to do in slavery. How they looked at me in the same embarrassed way I looked at my teachers when they talked about slavery. I called out sick from tutoring the next day. I needed a race day off.

I turned over to get some sun on my back and flipped on the radio. As if on cue, a popular female rapper's latest hit blared out. In it, she rapped that light skin was passé and that brown-skinned girls like her were the "in thing." Suddenly it felt like 1988 all over again.

My husband stepped into our backyard and sat down next to me.

"Listen to this song. Just a few more UV rays and I'll be in fashion, baby," I said, shaking my head. The song had embarrassed me into getting up. I'd just have to be light and proud.

Before I could gather up my towel and tanning oil, my husband grabbed my arm.

"What are you going to do if our daughter comes out blond-haired and blue-eyed and is late for one of your events because she's tanning to look more like her mom?"

I couldn't believe I'd never thought of that before. Probably because we had just gotten married and planning that had been enough stress for me. (How do you know what kind of pots to register for when you don't even know how to cook?) My husband was right, though. We could have a blond-haired blue-eyed child. There were all kinds of recessive genes lurking in our DNA.

By American racial classification, my husband is not biracial, but his family photos look like the covers of World History text-books. His grandmother and her long Native American hair, his cousins who look like they could be anything *but* black. Even his last name, my new one, is a mixture of cultures. His grandfather was a black Jamaican who didn't want to emigrate to the States with two marks against him—black man with an Irish name—so he added an "A" to McCalla and changed it to MacCalla, a tradi-tional Scottish surname.

I shuddered at how I was going to decode all this for my chil-dren. Will kids at school tease them for being zebras even if they look white? It's the twenty-first century and there are barely any books out to help parents raise mixed-race children. There is *no* lit-erature to help two black-identifying parents raise a blond-haired, blue-eyed child. I'm not sure I have the patience to blaze new trails like my mother did.

I'd love to tell my children that race doesn't matter, or even that the race thing gets easier when you get older, but I don't want to lie to them. Unless the United States becomes remarkably different in twenty or so years, race still will matter and not to prepare them for that smacks of irresponsible parenting to me. Plus, I'm sure my children will catch me having a *where do I fit in?* moment. Even though I don't go through the agony of my formative years by try-ing on different races and religions in response to people's percep-tions of me, I still have a bit of racial schizophrenia. When I'm with my family, I'm a black girl, shouting at racist news coverage, fan-ning people down in my mother and stepfather's church when they get the Holy Ghost. At home, in my predominantly white neighborhood, I choose to be racially neutral at times, flaunting my exoticness when people ask me what I am. *I'm everything* or *I'm American*, I say, enjoying the looks on their faces when they're caught between being politically correct and just dying to ask me to be more concrete, so they can place me in some kind of box.

I'm also a woman who can't eat in places that remind me of slavery. My husband loves this soup buffet chain out here called Souplantation. He has tried to convince me to try it, but I'm adamant. Why would they call it Soup *Plantation* unless they wanted to keep black people out?

However, for all my desires to stay away from things that remind me of pre–Civil War America, those same things are hanging right on my family tree. While researching my ancestors online, I found some cousins in Minnesota who have an award-winning polka band. One of their hit songs is titled "Cotton Fields." I am gathering up the nerve to contact them.

There is a part of me that still holds on to the positive things I acquired from hip-hop and Nation of Islam Lite. That part is certain that even if I choose a racial label other than black, it won't make me blind to injustice. I also know that I don't have to move to the hood to make a difference, but that I feel better when I'm doing *something* (hence the tutoring).

And, of course, I'm still partly that confused mixed girl, although now when my two identities clash, it often leads me to laugh at how surreal being biracial in America can be.

For example, on my first day of tutoring, the students automatically thought I was cool because my last name sounds exactly like the slang word rappers use for *nigga*. My *Nissel*.

"That's your real last name? That's hot," a girl said, before blowing a gum bubble bigger than her head.

"Yes, that's my real name," I replied. I refrained from telling her that *Nissel* is not only slang for *nigga*, it's German and one of the whitest last names around. *Save it for another lesson*, I thought to myself.

"We're going to be late for the plane!" my husband shouted. My tanning had screwed me. My foundation no longer matched my complexion. I gave up on trying to fix my face and helped Reuben load our pets into the car. Thankfully, their kennel was right near the airport.

Our dog, Woody, is a stubborn old mutt who did not want to share the seat with the cats. When he started barking at them, they responded by hissing at him and trying to claw through their carriers.

"Honey, we don't need to be talking about kids. Aren't these kids enough for now?" I said, struggling to hold our dog in the backseat.

Reuben wasn't listening to me. He was frustrated that we were running late. "I hate being late. People expect black people to be running late. I'm reinforcing the black stereotype, that we're always running on CP time!"

I understood, but I had to hold back a giggle because I didn't see the difference between his worry and the tanning he had gently admonished me for. It's all worry over something that has to do with skin color.

"I remember this one time, I was late for a dinner reservation and the hostess gives me this look, you know the look?" Reuben said as he stopped at a red light and again helped me get hold of our ninety-pound mutt to keep him from jumping into the front seat. While I was still settling Woody, the light changed and my husband pulled forward, causing the dog and me to knock skulls. I could feel the beginning of a headache. My husband started telling another story, about a time he was late to Little League when he was twelve and a racist coach used that as an excuse to bench him for two games.

I needed to focus on something else besides race and my headache. Plus, my husband drives like he's blind when he's afraid of being late. I reached for an old newspaper lying on the floor and opened it to the World section. The feature story detailed the sky-rocketing rates of bulimia and anorexia among Black South African teenage girls. *Really? Black girls from the motherland?* My mind wandered to what ethnicity box a white South African who immigrated to America would check off on the census. Technically, he'd be African American.

"I remember when we were the only black family in La Jolla. I used to get pulled over so much, I seriously thought about getting a bumper sticker that said I LIVE HERE, OFFICER," my husband said, eyeing a police cruiser.

I tried to laugh, but my headache was getting worse. I needed a break. Just one day of not thinking about race. But I knew it was impossible. There will always be police who stare at my husband and me in our own neighborhood, just like there will always be check boxes to fill out. I still have trouble finding a hair salon, and I doubt I will ever have to stop explaining to people what race I am. The other day, a white person at work told me that my opinion on a black character didn't count because I'm "barely black." I wasn't sure if he was joking, but I went into the bathroom and cried with my head between my legs, where I noticed a new mole. I have skin cancer! I thought. Maybe I *am* barely black—I'm going to die from a white-person disease! I went to my desk and Googled "skin cancer and black people." The first result was Bob Marley. I never knew he died of a malignant melanoma. I also didn't know his father was white. No one would dare call him barely black.

Still, with my head throbbing and the dog barking, I decided to take the rest of the day off from thinking about race. For the rest of the day, I wouldn't care if I was black enough or white enough. I gave up.

Suddenly my husband slammed on the brakes to avoid hitting the car in front of us, which had stopped for no reason. I braced myself, preparing for a hit from behind. Instead, the car behind us swerved around us and pulled up to my side of the car. The driver rolled down his window. I rolled down mine.

The driver, a middle-aged white man in a business suit, studied Reuben and me for a brief moment and yelled, "Where did you learn how to drive? Go back to Mexico!"

I laughed so hard, I screamed. My headache suddenly went away. The man looked confused. *You're supposed to be insulted,* the look on his face said. If he only knew that he had insulted us with one of the few ethnicities we have no ties to.

Well, I wanted a day without thinking about being black or white. I never thought about *Mexican*. I laughed again. Reuben started laughing, too. This made the driver even more pissed. He flipped us the bird, still looking for an explanation of why we were cracking up.

"I'm Italian!" I yelled out, through my laugh.

Reuben and I pulled off. We rode the laughter that only racial insanity can provide all the way to the airport.

Acknowledgments

To the Nissels, the MacCallas, and the Marshalls, for putting up with me and my deadlines. Thank you in advance for not disowning me because of anything contained in these pages.

To my agent Andy McNicol, whose enthusiasm kept me going. I couldn't have done this without you. To Marc Provissiero at William Morris, for keeping me safe in Hollywood. Thanks for signing me even though I was "incredibly naïve and green." You're more than my Hollywood superagent. You're my older brother, my friend, my cousin Vinnie (smile).

To Bill Lawrence and Randall Winston, for making the cutthroat entertainment business chockful o' fun! I would be lost without you guys (yes, especially you, Bill). I feel too dorky to tell you how much I appreciate you in person (yes, I especially appreciate you, Bill).

To Melody Guy for everything. You changed my life with one e-mail. You're like a good virus! Thank you!

To Brian McLendon, Benjamin Dreyer, Jennifer Jones, Danielle Durkin, and Janet Wygal, for working your tails off even when I was holding things up.

To the Mesa Refuge Writer's Retreat for understanding that writers need a place without a television or a phone.

To the *Scrubs* writers for being so much smarter and more witty than me that I've lost my ego and developed a stutter.

To Tommi Crump for being the strongest, most supportive homegirl in the world.

To Neal Brennan for your brutal honesty, support, and patience.

To Uhuru Smith, Shani Lee, and Tanya McCrae for being born cool and mixed and for helping me laugh and pick out the right hair products.